RE-ENTREPRENEURING

RE-ENTREPRENEURING

*How organizations can reignite
their entrepreneurial spirit*

ROLAND BERGER PARTNERS

Co-editors: Charles-Edouard Bouée
and Stefan Schaible

BLOOMSBURY BUSINESS
LONDON • NEW YORK • OXFORD • NEW DELHI • SYDNEY

BLOOMSBURY BUSINESS
Bloomsbury Publishing Plc
50 Bedford Square, London, WC1B 3DP, UK
1385 Broadway, New York, NY 10018, USA

BLOOMSBURY, BLOOMSBURY BUSINESS and the Diana logo are
trademarks of Bloomsbury Publishing Plc

First published in Great Britain 2019

Cover design by Eleanor Rose
Cover images: Chilli pepper © Suchart Doyemah / EyeEm / Getty images;
Bell pepper © Yevgen Romanenko / Getty Images

A catalogue record for this book is available from the British Library.

A catalog record for this book is available from the Library of Congress.

ISBN: HB: 978-1-4729-4824-3
        ePDF: 978-1-4729-4823-6
        eBook: 978-1-4729-4825-0

Typeset by RefineCatch Limited, Bungay, Suffolk
Printed and bound in Great Britain

To find out more about our authors and books visit www.bloomsbury.com and
sign up for our newsletters.

Dedicated to all the Roland Berger partners who have made re-entrepreneuring part of what we do every day and helped our clients succeed. Without you this book would not have been possible. Thank you.
– Charles-Edouard and Stefan

CONTENTS

PREFACE

In today's fast-paced world, a half-century is a long time. It is many lifetimes rolled into one. And this fact came to light when discussions began within Roland Berger, our consultancy firm, about how to celebrate the 50th anniversary in these days. The first few suggestions were predictable: we could mark our Golden Jubilee with a big party for current employees, their families, and our alumni. Or we could produce a glossy book, telling the story of our first 50 years with pictures of our people, beginning with our founder and progressing through the subsequent generations to ourselves.

Fifty years is a long time. We have added many feathers to our cap, weathered many storms and come out stronger. The Roland Berger of today is not the same as the Roland Berger of yester-years. The conversation took a more serious turn when someone asked what had changed in the half-century since our founder had set out his stall as a consultant for German organizations re-establishing themselves in the aftermath of World War 2.

We saw the period as consisting of several waves of change: the globalization wave of the 1970s, the personal computer wave of the 1980s, the mobile phone and Internet wave of the 1990s, the wave of the smartphone and the 'platform' business model in the first decade of the new millennium, and the current wave, which cannot yet be characterized, but which could be seen in some ways as a prelude to the coming age of artificial intelligence.

There was also a world of difference between the kind of work we did for clients, such as the German tourism group TUI, in the firm's early days and the kind of work we have been doing recently for clients such as Chinese smartphone suppliers OPPO/Vivo.

This led to the question of what, if anything, had stayed the same during Roland Berger's first 50 years.

The idea that led to our decision to write this book was that in helping organizations to preserve and create value we have been concerned, since the beginning, with the sources and uses of human energy.

Organizations have lives of their own that transcend those of the individuals who comprise them. But without the energy of the individuals who pass through them, they could not act, or react, to their constantly changing environments and the successive waves of change. This energy takes many forms, ranging from human passions for quality, elegance, speed and lean-ness, to qualities such as determination, loyalty, resilience and a refusal to take things as they are for granted.

Of all the forms of human energy that give life and vigour to organizations, entrepreneurial energy, the search for, and pursuit of, new opportunities to create value, is the prime mover. It gives birth to organizations in the first place, and is the only kind of energy that can renew and refresh an organization when changes in its environment demand an adaptive response.

Although we didn't always recognize it at the time, we realized that in most cases, it was this powerful entrepreneurial energy, which loosens and re-shapes, that we had been using in our assignments for companies, national and local governments, and non-governmental organizations (NGOs).

We didn't conclude from this, however, that we or our clients were 'entrepreneurs' in the normal sense of the word. In popular culture, the archetypal entrepreneur is a free agent who starts his or her own business either from scratch or as a spin-off or spin-out from an existing organization. Entrepreneurial energy in this personified form was not available to us or our clients, which are usually established organizations. But although we ourselves were not entrepreneurs, we realized that during assignments we and our clients often adopt the entrepreneurial outlook and behave in ways that have the hallmarks of entrepreneurialism.

It seemed to us that, without being conscious of doing so, we and our clients had succeeded in overcoming daunting obstacles by reaching back to the organization's origins, recapturing the then-dominant entrepreneurial outlook, and bringing it to bear on the challenges of today. We had managed to detach entrepreneurship and entrepreneurial energy from the person of the entrepreneur.

If we could bottle it and apply it at will, we would have the equivalent of an elixir of corporate youth that could be injected into organizations that were struggling to adapt to their changing environments. We had the impression that the need for such a tonic had been growing in recent years, because of what we call the VUCA factors or qualities (Volatility, Uncertainty, Complexity and Ambiguity) that have come to characterize the modern environment.

This book is an attempt to distil this entrepreneurial energy by looking back and re-interpreting some of the work that our more than 200 partners, 2,500 consultants with help of all our employees, and thousands of alumni have done for clients over the past half-century. We don't claim we are the only firm to use this energy, but we believe that we are among the first to recognize it for what it is: a juvenile form of creative energy that gets organizations going in the first place, but which they tend to lose access to as they develop.

The idea of 're-entrepreneuring', as we call these injections of entrepreneurial energy, was triggered by the chance combination of developments and circumstances. The 50th anniversary discussions were part of it. At the same time, interest in the 'Light Footprint Management' model we had proposed in 2013 (0.1), which urged organizations to recapture the agility of their youth, remained high. Third, we had been having some success in the market, with a new approach to re-structuring that we had called 'entrepreneurial re-structuring'.

These three themes came together in discussions with partners working in various industries. They focused attention on our own origins and on the idea of looking back to when organizations were younger, smaller and lighter on their feet, for inspiration about how to move forwards. Partners came up with many examples of where this general approach had been taken, some of which are described in the pages that follow. They emphasized that it wasn't a matter of literally going back and starting again. It was a matter of re-discovering entrepreneurial energy, and applying it to the current situation. Re-entrepreneuring differs from traditional consulting in that it is not a prescription or a remedy, but a re-awakening of dormant faculties, much as immunotherapies awaken immune systems.

The prefix 're-' in words such as re-structuring, re-forming, re-viewing and re-inventing, seemed an important theme to us, because it conveyed a sense of returning, and repeating an action that had been done before. If 'entrepreneuring' is what people do when they create organizations out of nothing, 're-entrepreneuring' is the application of the same creativity to assets and capabilities that already exist. It is re-arranging these assets and capabilities so that they can be used to seize new opportunities, and confront new challenges. From there, it was a small step to the conclusion that, to adapt to a VUCA world, organizations must learn the art of 're-entrepreneuring'.

This book is a collaboration – a joint exploration by members of a large global consulting firm of the implications for modern organizations of current trends and adaptive pressures. It is the creature of our own entrepreneurial energy, as we adapt ourselves, and our services to clients, to the threats and opportunities that lie in wait for all of us. Before we end, we would like to express our deep gratitude towards Tom Lloyd who helped us sift through nearly 50+ complex case studies and articulate the ideas presented in this book.

Charles-Edouard Bouée and Stefan Schaible

Introduction

A new way to be

The origin of practically every tangible or intangible artefact of the modern world, from the wheel to the smartphone, can be traced back to an entrepreneurial act. Entrepreneurial acts are rare, and account for a tiny fraction of all acts, but they're the engine of all progress and the source of all novelty.

Entrepreneurial acts are not, as they have often been assumed to be pure invention. They're best seen as insights into how ideas or objects that have already been thought of, or already exist, can be rearranged, reconfigured or recombined to create something new and valuable. The people of the late Neolithic period (*c.* 4,000 BCE) were already familiar with discs (of wood or stone) and round tree trunks, when what we may call an entrepreneur saw the two could be combined to create wheels and axles.

Some have suggested this ability to spot new possibilities in rearrangements of what already exists, what Israel Kirzner called 'entrepreneurial alertness', is such an important contributor to economic progress that it should be treated as a fourth 'factor of production', alongside land, labour and capital. Although it would be hard to incorporate entrepreneurial alertness as a key variable in the theory of the firm, the basic idea is sound.

Entrepreneurial activity is the fuel of economic progress, in the same way as mutation is the fuel of evolution. Given its value to societies, economies and organizations, it seems fair to assume we will always need more of it.

There is, of course, plenty of entrepreneurial activity going on in the corporate undergrowth. Most of it comes to nothing or to very little, but here and there a sapling will take root and grow into a giant tree. It is assumed, however, that in the development of an organization, the time for entrepreneurial activity is right at the beginning. And thus, entrepreneurial thinking becomes part of the DNA that the founders embed into the organization when it comes into existence. The organizational DNA, a nebulous term to describe the unconscious rules that make each organization unique, defines how a company thinks, acts, behaves and views opportunities and challenges. Once an organization is established, things change: qualities that were virtues in its ante- and neo-natal stages become vices and the entrepreneurial founders must cede control to professional managers who can nurture the fruits of their original vision efficiently.

It follows from this that, as organizations grow, they become more ordered and disciplined, and their focus shifts from novelty to incremental improvement. Such an environment is not conducive to entrepreneurial thinking. Entrepreneurial thinking may be tacitly discouraged because it can create novelty, and novelty is a threat to established organizations with large market shares.

Entrepreneurial activity is stimulated by uncertainty, and by a lack of discipline. Established organizations farming brands and franchises seek to achieve stability, maintain discipline, and pay very close attention to the details. There is insufficient slack in a modern, 'lean' organization for the entrepreneurial interplay of speculation and experimentation.

This book takes issue with this view of the world.

It argues that different approaches are required when the environment changes, and that the time when incumbent organizations could insulate themselves effectively from volatile, uncertain, complex and ambiguous (VUCA) external environments is past. Organizations must no longer aspire to be oases of calm in the shifting sands of the global economy. They must adapt to, and become at one with, the market, by reviving the entrepreneurial outlook of their founders. They must reactivate the entrepreneurial DNA embedded in the organization by the founders.

Cultures that unknowingly discourage entrepreneurial thinking by focusing their employees' attention too narrowly on preserving what they have exposed themselves to risk being overtaken by events. They will miss opportunities to innovate, and fail to spot emerging threats in the form of new products, services or business models.

It is often assumed that some people are 'entrepreneurial' and others are not. If this were true, a farmer organization could only become a hunter organization by replacing personnel. The challenge of transforming a culture focused on preserving and farming into one focused on creating and hunting may not be as formidable as it seems at first sight, however.

It is an over-simplification to say that some people have the entrepreneur gene and some do not. Some may be more entrepreneurial than others, but we can all be entrepreneurs in organizations that foster the entrepreneurial outlook. It has more to do with the way of thinking encouraged by the culture than inherent differences in talent or aptitude.

Having made the case for reviving the entrepreneurial outlook in large, established organizations, we will then go on to examine how the entrepreneurial outlook can be deployed and used.

As noted above, entrepreneurs create novelty by combining old ideas and objects in new configurations. In the pages that follow, we will show with the help of case studies how the entrepreneurial approach can be applied to all organizations, from governments, to processes, and at all levels, to create new value of all kinds.

Since the activities we prescribe are rearrangements, rather than pure invention, many will begin with the prefix 're', such as recombine, reconfigure, reconstitute, recraft, redesign, reform, reframe, reimagine, remake, reorganize, replace, reshape, restore, restructure, rethink, review. The 're' prefix signifies 'back' or 'again'. The French term '*reculer pour mieux sauter*' ('to step back to go forward more strongly') encapsulates the idea perfectly.

The re-entrepreneuring approach corresponds, in some ways, to 'zero-based budgeting', although we will not be overly concerned with budgets or budgeting. The zero-base is the '*reculer*': the stepping back, to make a fresh start. The approach is also analogous to the 'system restore' feature in Microsoft Windows that allows users to change their computers' states to earlier points, before they were corrupted or became dysfunctional.

Entrepreneurs are lean and hungry. Most start with nothing or next to nothing and acquire substance, in the form of premises and people, reluctantly. The revival of entrepreneurial thinking in an established organization can, therefore, be expected to lead to a shedding of mass, through the adoption of a zero-based approach to everything, not just budgets. An entrepreneurial restructuring of an established organization will ask 'what are the minima required to serve customers well of premises, travel, energy inputs, people and other fixed costs?' – and will use the answers to such questions to build what we call an 'adapted' business model.

The entrepreneurial distaste for mass is an adaptive response to the modern environment where speed and agility are at a premium and mass makes organizations slow and cumbersome. The economies of scale that were the rationale for size are melting away now in the heat of evolving technology and bringing the dis-economies of scale to the fore. It is not mass that ensures success, it is impact.

And so the most massive incumbents might feel doomed. They are surrounded by nimbler rivals, sometimes from completely unrelated fields, who are constantly stealing a march over them. They feel like dinosaurs – massive, heavy, slow to move and even slower to evolve. But the reality is far less bleak. In their size, they might have hidden advantages even though they might not always see it that way. When the evolutionary pressure is on, they are likely to prove surprisingly adaptable. They are not, as they're often said to be and sometimes see themselves to be, powerless to defend themselves against more nimble tech-savvy new entrants and start-ups armed with the latest technology and so-called 'platform' business models. Despite what capital markets imply when assigning price–earnings multiples, the alleged weaknesses of conventional companies can be transformed into strengths when their assets and capabilities are seen through entrepreneurial eyes.

Israel Kirzner, who proposed the addition of 'entrepreneurial alertness' to the three factors of production, saw it as a kind of vision – an ability to see combinations of events, 'realized or prospective, which offer pure gain.' This is what entrepreneurs do and have done since the dawn of commerce.

This is not an academic book, but it covers ground that has been much discussed by management academics since it was sketched out by Joseph Schumpeter in *Capitalism, Socialism and Democracy* (Harper & Brothers, 1942). It would be remiss of us, therefore, not to put our arguments in the context of the academic discussion.

The academic debate is concerned with the balance between two kinds of activity: 'explorative' and 'exploitative'. Explorative (which means 'exploratory') corresponds to what some call 'hunter' activity and, roughly, with what we call entrepreneurial activity. Exploitative activity corresponds to 'farmer' activity and what we call managerial activity.

The academics take it as read that to survive and thrive over time, an organization must engage in both kinds of activity. (0.2) Those that do are said to be 'ambidextrous' (in common usage, this means having equal facility in the use of both left and right hands). We agree that organizations must be 'ambidextrous' in this sense. We argue, however, that the optimal balance between 'explorative' and 'exploitative' activity depends partly on the environment. We say organizations need to engage in more explorative activity, if they are to remain adapted to a more VUCA environment.

The literature discusses three ways to achieve the quality of ambidexterity: 'sequential', in which periods when one is dominant alternate with periods when the other is dominant; 'structural', in which the activities are simultaneous, but separate (as when an organization confines its explorative activity within a separate R&D department); and 'contextual', where both activities happen at the level of the individual, rather than the organization.

We take the view that sequential ambidexterity is the default pattern – that most organizations emerge from an initial burst of entrepreneurial (explorative) energy, which is then followed by a period of consolidation in which the fruits of the entrepreneurial energy are harvested (exploitative activity), and must then return to explorative activity when the harvest is in. We argue that this default pattern begs questions about the frequency of the sequence and that in a VUCA world the frequency must be so high to maintain adaptation, that the activities must be effectively simultaneous.

The academic literature also distinguishes between useful and novel outcomes of explorative activity. This distinction is not of interest to us, because our 'unit of innovation', so to speak, is the 'entrepreneurial opportunity', which is by our definition both useful and novel. However, recent research showing that innovation is more likely to be useful if it is the result of contextual, rather than structural, explorative activity supports our view that energy released by re-entrepreneuring flows from the bottom, up.

The star actor in our drama is something we call entrepreneuring, a way of thinking and acting like an entrepreneur. Although the environments for organizations of all kinds have been changing out of all recognition in the past half-century or so, the prime mover of progress (0.3) has always been, and remains, the act of entrepreneuring.

The book begins in Chapter 1 by arguing that the way to adapt and remain adapted to the modern VUCA environment is to step back and revive the initial burst of entrepreneurial energy from which the organization originally emerged. It characterizes TUI Group, the German travel company, as the creature of both entrepreneurial and managerial activity.

With the help of case studies, Chapter 2 shows how a major discontinuity in an organization's history, such as a merger or a privatization, is a rare opportunity to flip the organization into a more collectively entrepreneurial state of mind.

Chapter 3 explains how organizations can be re-entrepreneured, both due to and in the absence of existential threats, by launching what we call an 'entrepreneurial re-structuring', based on an 'adapted business model'. The 'adapted business model', the business model you would choose if you were starting from scratch today, plays an important role in our argument. Few business models are adapted, because the moment a business model is implemented, it will begin to drift out of fit with the environment.

In Chapter 4, the general applicability of re-entrepreneuring is demonstrated by showing, with references to Germany's reunification in 1990, how governments can improve the performance of their economies by liberating hitherto latent entrepreneurial energy. It argues that, although it is true entrepreneurs need to be motivated by the prospect of rewards, the rewards need not be material and it is, therefore, wrong to assume the public sector is, of necessity, an entrepreneur-free zone.

Chapter 5 shows how the power of entrepreneurial thinking can transform organizations, as the iPod and iPhone transformed Apple, and that sometimes such transformations can be so complete that no trace of the origins of the organization remain.

Our attention in Chapter 6 returns to business models, their relationships with cultures, and how 'adapted' business models and the re-entrepreneuring ethos that is associated with them, tend to spread up and down value chains and throughout ecosystems.

Chapter 7 focuses on new businesses, born into the VUCA world and so better adapted to it than older businesses, and shows how they have retained to maturity 'juvenile' entrepreneurial qualities.

In Chapter 8 we describe a remarkable re-entrepreneuring project in the not-for-profit sector.

The book ends, in Chapter 9, with a discussion of some of the key principles of re-entrepreneuring.

1

Reculer pour mieux sauter

All companies begin with an entrepreneurial act, but successful companies usually lose that youthful impulse over time. As the firm becomes an institution, managers' concerns typically shift to preserving the company's franchise. They begin to pursue a more conservative strategy, doing more of whatever won them their initial success. They add tangible assets (plant, buildings, cash, inventory, etc.), develop intangible assets (intellectual property, reputation, structure and culture), and extend their distinctive ecosystem of like-minded partners and vendors.

Sooner or later, however, the times in which the company found its original niche begin to change. Maybe the market declines and a set of key customers move on. Maybe new competition reduces the profitability of the old business model. Or maybe technology eliminates the profitability of an entire industry, destroying the value of formerly prized assets and expertise. In any case, executives realize that their winning formula does not seem to win quite so often any more.

Now the company must reinvent itself. If it is to thrive again, managers will need to find some entrepreneurial instincts within themselves or recover a dormant entrepreneurial impulse from the company's youth. Then, looking at their current assets and liabilities, and after thinking through the true mission of their business, they make a decision about where the firm will go from here. We call this process re-entrepreneuring.

The French saying *reculer pour mieux sauter* (step back, to go forward more strongly) sums up the idea. To cross a stream, you don't step into it; you retrace your steps, run at it and jump across. Similarly, we find that despite all the new opportunities created by technology, the solutions to the key problems the organization faces today or anticipates facing tomorrow often lie in its past. In particular, they lie with those entrepreneurial qualities that were considered relevant at an earlier stage of the organization's development but have atrophied in maturity.

Entrepreneuring by its nature is a youthful act. Howard Stevenson, Emeritus Sarofim-Rock Professor at Harvard Business School, defines 'entrepreneurship' as a 'pursuit of opportunity without regard to resources currently controlled'. Entrepreneurs 'see an opportunity and don't feel constrained from pursuing it, because they lack resources. They're used to making do without resources'. (1.1)

Re-entrepreneuring is an older and wiser version of the same act. In many ways, it is a braver one, as the leaders making the new bets understand more clearly all that is at risk. It entails nothing less than the innovative realignment of an existing set of assets and processes in pursuit of a new opportunity or to create new value.

As we shall see in the following case of TUI, the German travel giant, sometimes companies survive this phase by acquiring new assets. Other times, as with Apple and the iPod, they win that new lease on life by creating new products. Either way, the essential quality of re-entrepreneuring is that it is not a matter of thinking 'outside the box' – it is about thinking *with* the box, applying the company's existing assets and distinctive qualities to a new purpose, using the box itself as a stepping stone that will carry the company across a difficult time to a better time.

The emergence of TUI

The Great Depression tanked many businesses, but those that survived went on to prosper. One unlikely survivor was Dr Tigges-Fahrten, a holiday company founded in 1928, just before the stock market crash. The recession was not the best of times for leisure and entertainment businesses, but Tigges-Fahrten sailed through by smartly focusing on budget tours. It wasn't smooth sailing all along though, and the business had to go into a hiatus during World War 2. Despite the adverse circumstances, it continued to adapt its strategy and by 1953 it had organized its first air tour and, over the next decade, it had diversified well beyond Europe and organized its first world tour.

At this time, the firm came to realize that the future of tourism was in air travel, and that this would demand a different kind of business organization. Buses were cheap. Airplanes were not: air tours were cash-intensive because of the need to pre-book seats for chartered flights. But to succeed, substantial financial and organizational resources would be needed to operate on a scale the market had begun to demand. Only a larger company could maintain the necessary level of working capital to keep the business afloat. To prepare for these new conditions, Tigges merged with Touropa and Scharnow-Reisen and, later, a long-standing joint venture partner, Hummel Reisen. In 1968, the four companies rebranded themselves as 'Touristik Union International' (TUI).

The team designed a robust management structure that would play to the strengths of the constituent companies' leaders, and the TUI group adopted a full-range approach to cover all segments of the market.

Each constituent company concentrated on those segments in which it had a competitive advantage – Tigges: study trips, expeditions and adventure tours; Hummel, Scharnow, Touropa: sport trips; Scharnow, Touropa: health and convalescent trips. The aim was to sharpen the focus of the group companies, reduce competition between them and, by working together, offer a range of products that covered the most lucrative segments of the market.

By adopting the holding company model, TUI aimed to achieve substantial cost savings by taking over administrative tasks from the four companies so that they could focus their attention on the operations. Central units were formed for accounting, review, tax and materials purchases. A group marketing department, supplying market research, advertising, and sales promotion services was also developed. As these services did not differentiate each company's offering, they could be centralized to save costs.

But differentiation was still necessary in the product ranges, and so the managing directors of the individual brands retained the responsibility for their tour line-ups. In this way, TUI distinguished between 'initial' (entrepreneurial) creativity, which was the responsibility of the group companies, and 'selective' creativity, such as brochures and advertisements, which fell under the purview of central management.

The merger worked. In 1969, annual customer numbers exceeded a million for the first time, and services and product lines were extended.

Over the next two decades, TUI continued to expand its portfolio of high-quality travel products and services. In 1970, it formed its travel services division, TUI Service, and substantially increased the range of services offered by its operators. The broad spectrum of packaged and individual trips by air, train, car and ship was complemented by new holiday formats ranging from club holidays and stays at country farms, to trips to nudist beaches for sunbathers, tennis and sport centres, and a special youth travel programme, 'twen-tours'.

The company launched a joint venture as well that would prove significant in the coming years. In 1971, TUI, Germany's airline, Lufthansa, and the Bundesbahn (the state-owned rail network) formed a joint venture to develop a new electronic booking system.

In the early 1970s, TUI also stepped into the hotels and hospitality business by laying the foundations of the Robinson Hotels brand along with Steigenberger Hotelgesellschaft. The first Robinson Club – the Jandia Playa – was set up in Fuerteventura in 1971. Then in 1972, TUI acquired Iberotel, the Spanish hotel chain.

This 'merger strategy' proved to be the right one. By creating communalities of challenges and solutions, it allowed TUI to stand out from the mass in a more and more competitive market. Several decades later, TUI has changed, of course. But it is still operating in this 're-entrepreneuring' mode, relying on effective governance and efficient back-office functions, and with a strong focus on content, at a time when tourists are looking for authentic and personal experiences.

Another company that has been strong with its re-entrepreneurial instincts is Apple. Apple entered its 're-entrepreneuring' stage shortly after founder Steve Jobs walked back into Apple's headquarters in January 1997, 12 years after being fired as CEO. (1.2)

First, he took a step back. He cut Apple's product line back by 70 per cent, eliminating problematic products such as the Newton, a precursor of the Palm Pilot and the other Personal Digital Assistant electronic note-keepers, and cut the workforce as well by about 3,000 employees, out of a total of 11,000. 'Deciding what not to do is as important as deciding what to do,' he later explained. 'It's true for companies, and it's true for products.'

Then, he took a surprising step forward, one that would transform both the computer business and the entire music industry – but not without a little wobbling on its back foot first.

In the late 1990s, the popularity of online music exploded, as consumers began to take advantage of the digitalization of music that had begun in the 1980s with the mass adoption of the compact disc (CD). College students, and later other music listeners, learned to share music files. Napster and a number of file-sharing sites attracted millions of followers. In the year 2000 alone, 320 million blank CDs were sold in the US, which consumers used to store music they had 'ripped' from Napster and other file-sharing sites. A new era in digital entertainment had begun, but without Apple.

The catch-up campaign began with the addition of a CD burner on the iMac, but that was not enough. Jobs wanted an MP3 player. To the techno-zen culture nurtured by Jobs, the MP3 players then on the market were clunky, ugly and seriously lacking in storage capacity. Jobs and his colleagues listened to a lot of music and knew what 'good' would look like in an MP3 player: elegant, easy to use, and capable of storing a 1,000-song playlist. As he had with the Macintosh computer nearly 20 years earlier, Jobs and his team looked at the clumsy, inelegant technology and saw a transformational opportunity.

This time around, however, they had more than the eye for design and obsession for quality they had in 1984: they realized that they already owned some of the key elements of an entire new music ecosystem.

Apple already had the key component in FireWire (an IEEE 1394 serial port), which it had developed a decade earlier to transfer files from one device to another. It was just a matter of reaching back, and deploying it in new applications.

Apple had also already launched its own music service, through another act of re-entrepreneuring: the company had found a music file-sharing start-up run by three members of its alumni network. They recognized that SoundJam could be designed to be more attractive than Napster and the other pirate music sites. Apple acquired and then rebranded SoundJam as iTunes in early 2001, releasing it as an application free to all Mac users.

It also went beyond the other file-sharing sites at the time by creating a legal market for online music that hadn't really existed before, giving Apple a new role in the music business as a retailer.

The decision to develop what became the iPod was a violation of a time-honoured management axiom that a company should stick to its knitting. But Jobs and his team understood that Apple's true value was not as a computer company, but as a maker of consumer-friendly digital tools. By going back to Jobs' initial understanding that consumers would respond to elegant, easy-to-use design in an aesthetically pleasing appliance, and that Apple's core value lay in delivering such beautiful machines, they found a vast new opportunity, setting the company on a new path that led straight to the iPad and then the iPhone and the iPhone Appstore, creating two vast platforms for digital content that completely realigned electronics, media and entertainment.

At some point, almost every company faces a variation of the kind of challenge faced by TUI and Apple – a changing world in which they are on the verge of losing their niche. What is different today is that even relatively young companies are facing what tended to be more of a mid-life crisis.

Vijay Govindarajan and Anup Srivastava, professors at Dartmouth College's Tuck School of Business, analysed all 29,688 firms that listed from 1960 through 2009 and found that failure is more common in newly listed firms as opposed to older ones. They write, 'A company listed before 1970 had a 92 percent chance of surviving the next five years, compared to just 63 percent for a company listed between 2000 and 2009.' (1.3)

Reasons are not hard to find: the environment is changing faster than ever. With the arrival of the personal computer (PC) in the 1980s, the Internet, the smartphone, and the exponential growth of data substituted for the steam engine, we find ourselves in the throes of a similar transition in the adaptation of our organizations to their changing environment. And with artificial intelligence (AI) and further dramatic advances in microbiology just around the corner, the adaptive pressure can only become more intense.

Often, the effects of these pressures take a little while to make themselves felt. Not much happened in organizational design during the initial PC wave, when IBM and Hewlett-Packard were the pioneers, but new business models and organizational structures began to emerge when the baton passed to a host of 'IBM-compatible' new entrants, such as Compaq and Dell. The typical pattern, displayed by the railways in the nineteenth century and the automobile industry in the twentieth century, is an initial proliferation, followed by consolidation, as natural selection (competition) winnows the host of new entrants down to a few survivors (e.g. Apple and Microsoft, in this case).

The same pattern unfolded during the commercialization of the Internet. In this case, the novelty of the 'space' being colonized by the horde of new entrants led to more organizational innovation from the outset, but pioneers, such as AOL and Yahoo, didn't stay the course. The initial proliferation was christened the dotcom boom and culminated in the upstart new economy AOL acquiring a pillar of the old economy, Time Warner, in early 2000. The NASDAQ index peaked at 5,133 on 10 March 2000. The bursting of the dotcom bubble pushed the NASDAQ down 78 per cent by the end of 2002. In the tumult that followed, many companies simply vanished, while others saw their stocks plummet. Cisco, for instance, which in the year 2000 surpassed Microsoft to become the most valuable company in the world, saw its share price fall by a whopping 86 per cent after the dotcom bust.

The pioneers in the early days of mobile telephony too went through the same process. Motorola, Nokia, Blackberry and Ericsson began as the industry's leaders, but lost their way with the arrival of the smartphone, when Apple, then Samsung, Huawei, OPPO/Vivo and Xiaomi took over the market (see page 110).

It is safe to say that the same pattern of pioneering, followed by proliferation and consolidation, will probably repeat itself in the coming artificial intelligence revolution.

Are pioneers doomed to fall by the wayside as the products or markets they create are 'commoditized', or otherwise transformed, and their organizational structures or business models cease to be fit for purpose?

We do not believe so, but there is no denying that the adaptive pressure is increasing on all organizations, and it is clear that the traditional corporate structure is itself under pressure.

Advances in information and communication technologies in the 170 or so years since the modern company first made its appearance have reduced transaction and information costs almost to zero, and have dramatically increased the efficiency of inter-firm coordination. Some say that net transaction costs may now even be negative sometimes, because the connection costs less now than the value they add to a firm's network capital and reputational assets. At the same time, the growth of outsourcing, joint ventures, alliances, partnerships and other kinds of co-operation, which gives globalization its substance, suggests that, in some sectors, traditional top-down organizing no longer makes much sense.

What next? As Nobel Laureate molecular biologist Jacques Monod said, evolution in nature is driven by a combination of 'chance and necessity'. (1.4) Today, partnering and co-operation have become so common that it makes more sense to think in terms of business ecosystems, rather than integrated companies, consisting of value-chain neighbours and trusted suppliers and customers. Each member pursues its own goals, but in so doing imparts a collective direction to the ecosystem as a whole, much as ants exhibit 'swarm intelligence'. Some have suggested that an ecosystem of this kind, consisting of Microsoft and the PC clone makers, such as Compaq and Dell, unintentionally destroyed IBM's PC business.

Another development that is undermining the cultural intensity of large companies and other organizations is the increase in the mobility of their personnel. Employers began to repudiate the old job-for-life social contract that used to be the norm in the corporate world in the downsizings and delayerings of the early 1990s. The consequence is that few people now envision their career as a steady climb up one organization's hierarchy. The increased mobility of managers is also attributable in part to a proliferation of specialities – finance, operations, marketing, manufacturing, ICT, HR – which have led to a shift in focus away from loyalty to an organization to one's profession.

The loss of control over individuals has followed in step with a loss of control in most industries and economies of their market. As trade expands, the market power of individual companies falls, and instruments of market control, such as IP protection, have become less effective.

Over the past few years, a new shift in power has been underway and, again, large established companies have been conspicuous by their absence, with Airbnb, Alibaba, Didi Chuxing, Facebook, PayPal, Tencent, Twitter and Uber taking the lead. Digital technologies favour entrepreneurs, because they allow them to scale-up rapidly through network effects, adopt agile business models and keep costs low.

How should an incumbent respond?

The word entrepreneur is a noun: to be more specific, a person. If real entrepreneurs were as thin on the ground as most people believe, it would be fruitless to suggest, as we intend, that they are a solution to the problem of adaptation, at the firm-level. They can help an economy to adapt, but if they are rare, they are unlikely to be available to a particular organization.

But suppose entrepreneur was a verb. What would it mean 'to entrepreneur' and how much 'entrepreneuring' is, or could be going on?

Although serial entrepreneurs addicted to the new and the risky are rare, everyone can adopt the entrepreneurial outlook or approach when contexts permit or circumstances demand.

The interesting question for organizations, then, is not how few full-blooded entrepreneurs there are, but how common, how accessible and how easily invoked are their approaches, outlooks and qualities.

From this we can derive a definition of 'entrepreneuring' for our purposes: *A way of thinking and acting that takes nothing for granted, is unconstrained by any resource considerations and seeks opportunities not previously identified to create value as quickly as possible.*

The argument we will make in this book is that the winners in the world we live and work in today will be organizations that focus their entrepreneurial instincts in a way that does not disregard their current assets. Jobs' return helped invoke the entrepreneurial instincts that lay buried deep in Apple's DNA but had been lost over time. Tigges never hesitated to face the changing travel market and adjust itself to meet its needs. But it need not involve a reclaiming of the past so much as clear-eyed sense of the company's present.

Many organizations mistakenly assume that in order to progress they must look at reviving the start-up mind-set, and ignoring the strengths and capabilities they have grown over time. As a result, they experiment with start-ups. They either develop initiatives such as incubators or intrapreneurship programmes, or invest through corporate venture funds in promising start-ups. Both ways have important drawbacks. In the first case, 'intrapreneurs' often lack a real sense of autonomy that allows them not only to improve the existing models, but also to explore new growth opportunities. Conversely, externally, direct investment in promising start-ups does not rely on the company's strengths, and that then leads up to another challenge: that of integrating the entrepreneurial ventures into the main organization.[1]

You won't win by forgetting who you are now and 'going back to the garage,' but you might if you take a clear look at your company, its circumstances, and your opportunity with candour and a discerning eye.

SUMMARY

- Reaching back can illuminate the way forward.
- 'Entrepreneuring' means to act in an unconstrained way and create value that did not exist before.
- We can all engage in entrepreneuring in the right circumstances.
- 'Re-entrepreneuring' rejuvenates established organizations.
- It is the organization's primary adaptive mechanism in a volatile and uncertain environment.

2

Re-start

Finding opportunities in discontinuities

Not all acts of re-entrepreneuring involve reaching back to the beginning. Sometimes, a merger, a buyout or a privatization serves to ignite an entrepreneurial impulse, and can serve to send the enterprise on a new course.

Such opportunities can arise unexpectedly. For example, when a 2-year-old financial publication we will call *MoneyTalk* was judged by its owners to be a failed experiment and shut down, most of its staff of 30 or so pocketed their severance cheques and began looking for new jobs. But a small group of senior journalists was not ready to give up. They believed their magazine had only failed because of mismanagement. After convincing a group of backers that they could run the publication on a cost base almost 50 per cent lower than that of the failed magazine, they approached the owner with an offer to buy the title for a nominal sum. Their offer was accepted and the buyout group rehired half the staff.

They were unlike classical entrepreneurs – journalists, not managers, and had been pursuing the standard journalistic career path of moving from publication to publication. The announcement of closure confronted them with a choice: to go quietly to the next masthead, or try again where their former bosses had failed.

The threat of closure is not the only kind of discontinuity that can awaken a latent entrepreneurial outlook. A merger or an acquisition may also spark a new beginning. Mergers can do the same thing. Those managing a post-merger integration are often obliged to think about the enlarged business in ways that managers of the constituent businesses were unused to or had forgotten.

There are many forms of mergers, ranging from complete absorption of the target by the acquirer and casting the shreds of the former's culture to the winds, to a so-called merger of equals, where the role of 'acquirer' is not assigned, according to relative size (however measured) or relative profitability, but for geographical or fiscal expediency.

But mergers are not easy: a number of studies have concluded that roughly 50 per cent, if not more, of all mergers and acquisitions fail. As with marriages, what looked appealing in theory does not always work out so well in practice; bringing two cultures together is seldom easy.

Mergers of equals may be the toughest of all to execute because the necessarily uncertain power dynamic makes the fusion even more daunting. At the same time, however, a merger between equals often presents the greatest opportunities for re-entrepreneuring. When two organizations with different entrepreneurial traditions are brought together successfully, a lot of value can be created – or lost, depending on how things are handled.

bibliotheca and 3M Library Systems: The best of both worlds

In the Spring of 2011, JP Morgan Chase's private equity division, One Equity Partners (OEP), merged three leading library services companies, Intellident of the UK, Integrated Technology Group of the US, and Bibliotheca of Switzerland into a single entity that would also be known as bibliotheca.

Although OEP initially saw bibliotheca's *raison d'être* to provide 'radio-frequency identification' (RFID) security and productivity technology to libraries, the private equity firm soon had a bigger vision: to turn the company into a global library services powerhouse. In 2012, the group acquired Trion AG, a leading European supplier of automated materials handling systems, which are heavy users of RFID, and in early 2015 it added Aturis Group, a supplier of library systems in the Netherlands, Belgium and Germany, to its portfolio. The company also acquired local industry specialists in Brazil and Korea and developed partnerships that extended its reach into Scandinavia.

By 2015, bibliotheca had developed into the second-largest player in the space when the opportunity emerged to acquire the library business of 3M.

In certain respects, it was a merger of opposites. bibliotheca was very entrepreneurial, and retained the attributes of a start-up culture. The leadership was hands-on and aggressive, and the culture very European, reflecting the company's Swiss and British heritage. 3M Library Systems' qualities reflected those of its conglomerate parent: it was very quality driven and technically excellent, but not always agile.

Instead of picking one company or the other as the template, management decided to take a re-entrepreneuring approach. The firm would reset the development clock, and treat the enlarged company as a start-up organization with a brand new multinational management team that drew members from each of the original companies, five nationalities in all. Shareholders and management wanted to build a dream team that could deliver the 'best of both worlds', combining the excellent products, processes and technology that 3M had brought to the merger with the growth ambitions and entrepreneurial energy of bibliotheca.

Speed was important, because the merger had been partly financed by debt and the new company's debt providers asked for quick stability and loan security. Disruption of the merged business was minimized through a sequential integration process, designed to permit both operations to continue as usual. Close attention was paid to the cultural differences between the companies and operating regions.

Acutely conscious of cultural sensitivities, the post-merger integration team wanted to make sure that, in the end, the merged entity would feel like a new company and all that would be left of bibliotheca would be the name. They opened a brand new office in Minneapolis to avoid an imposition of European processes on the larger American business. In addition, a governance was installed that combined European and US managerial traditions. One European practice they saw as important to keep was regular face-to-face meetings. They realized that meeting at a different bibliotheca location each month would foster mutual understanding among colleagues from both sides of the new company's family. These meetings have built greater trust between top managers, helping them to understand local challenges better. Following that, they developed a common leadership language, which has made it easier to drive a shared agenda on how to build a global, standardized technology platform. Also, the managers were able to achieve a consensus about how the new company would measure success. Although this might look like a lot of extra work at a time when they had many other pressing concerns, managers said that the global meetings actually strengthened and accelerated the change management process.

Having arrived on the same page, managers quickly identified and realized substantial opportunities to reduce the cost of goods sold and operating expenses as well as rationalizing their product portfolios.

Other opportunities also opened up after the merger. Thanks to their combined resources, the new team realized, they now had the scale to tackle a major opportunity that neither had dared attempt alone: conquering the growing Chinese market. Together, they could come up with the money and resources needed to enter China, a vast and growing market where neither bibliotheca nor 3M had made any headway.

Entering China became possible not just because of the new bibliotheca's greater scale, however, but because the new company's first development project had been to build a standardized, global technology platform. The team also understood from the start that offering high-quality, tailored solutions would be the key to sales to their institutional customers, chiefly state and local libraries and universities; the new bibliotheca's selling point in China would be value not price.

At the same time, an agile manufacturing model enabled them to manufacture hardware locally with components made elsewhere, allowing them to label products 'Made in China', which was another attractive feature for the buyers, who are mostly government-owned entities.

Two years later, the new bibliotheca has not only gained market share in its home markets in Europe and North America, it is now becoming a major library services provider in China – and it is growing. 'In China, we still have a way to go,' said one manager, 'but we have been successfully working towards establishing a credible presence in the market. We have our sights on being in the Top 3 within the next few years.'

Changes of state

In a merger of equals, the main post-merger integration challenges are to do with mutual adaptation within an environment the parties to the merger share and have been adapting to in the normal course of events. A different set of challenges face organizations that are obliged, sometimes against their will, to become a completely different kind of organization. An enterprise forced to move from the public to the private sector is like a colonist landing on a new planet who must adapt suddenly to new weather, new geology, and new flora and fauna.

But a privatization is also another opportunity for re-entrepreneuring, a moment when smart managers stop, step back ('*reculer*'), take stock and think in zero-based, entrepreneurial ways about how to fulfil their mission in a new context.

Deutsche Post: Staying relevant and competitive

In 1989, West Germany's Deutsche Bundespost was transformed into three state-owned businesses: Deutsche Bundespost Telekom for the telecommunications sector; Deutsche Bundespost Postbank for the banking business; and Deutsche Bundespost Postdienst for the postal services. The main goal of this transformation was to develop innovative, inexpensive telecommunications services to ensure that West Germany stayed competitive in the fast-growing sector. (2.1)

The regulatory and political aspects of the three businesses were separated from the managerial and operational aspects, new management and supervisory boards were formed, a council for infrastructure matters consisting of members of the two German parliamentary chambers, Deutscher Bundestag and Deutscher Bundesrat, was appointed to ensure the relevant federal ministry co-ordinated with the council, and the legal basis of the companies' customer relationships was converted from public to private law. A board of directors was also created to which the management board chairpersons of the three companies belonged. This so-called 'Post Reform I' prepared the way for the full privatization of Deutsche Bundespost later on. The following year, the challenge grew still greater, as these firms had to begin integrating the East German postal service as well into its privatized schema.

On January 1, 1995, Deutsche Bundespost Postdienst was renamed Deutsche Post (2.2), and registered as a company in Bonn. Like the other ex-Bundespost components, Postbank and Telekom, it remained state-owned, but more change was afoot.

Management now had to prepare for life in the private sector, to build a platform to operate as a private company, develop relationships with capital markets and, at the same time, deal with employees, who even in the privatized company would retain all the rights of civil servants.

A change management team was formed to implement the metamorphosis. They began the hard work of recrafting the bureaucracy, corporate governance, organizational structure, and the incentive system (to boost productivity and allow the company to compete on equal terms in the vital skills market).

The central cultural challenge was to transform 340,000 employees with the civil servant's outlook on life and work, into private sector employees, working under a profit-oriented incentive system and bottom-line focused managers.

Overall, the reaction was not positive. Most Deutsche Post people had originally joined Deutsche Post in the belief they would be civil servants with all the pros and cons that went with that status. A few managers and younger people saw opportunities for their own personal development in the private sector environment, but the institution, as a whole, was not motivated to move in that direction.

The change management team began with directives, but soon realized they needed to work bottom-up with the people if they wanted more than minimal change to occur. An engaged employee would be in a better position to see opportunities for process optimization than senior supervisors. One team member reflected later that this simple shift to encourage change from the bottom up was more important to the reinvention of Deutsche Post than all the other re-engineering and process optimization work it undertook.

Yet difficulties persisted – and persist, even today. Looking back, one change team member says he thought he and all his colleagues underestimated the time it takes to change people's behaviour and motivation. Even today, there are a few Deutsche Post employees who see themselves as civil servants and there were many employed at the time of the privatization who retired without ever having 'got' the private sector ethos.

Beyond the shift to bottom-up management, they also tried to encourage rivalry between different parts of the postal system through workshops and seminars. All of this was designed to help change the behaviour of employees who were still civil servants, in terms of their contracts of employment.

It helped that there was no alternative. Deutsche Post had to transform itself from a state-owned and state-run bureaucracy into a competitive, independent private sector company – the government had so decreed. The fact that the company has since performed well on stock markets is a testament to the quality of the groundwork done in the mid-1990s, before flotation.

In January 1998, a new postal law came into effect. It renewed Deutsche Post's statutory obligation to provide postal services in Germany and granted it the exclusive right to deliver most letters and addressed catalogues weighing under 200 grams until the end of 2002. Although still owned by the government and government-owned development bank Kreditanstalt für Wiederaufbau (KfW), in 1998, the entrepreneurial outlook was already well-established. Inefficient post offices were closing, and Deutsche Post began to expand into new markets such as direct marketing, in-house postal services for large corporations, electronic transfers of letters from financial institutions, and online shopping.

The company also widened its geographical horizons, and began to buy shares in ground parcel delivery firms in Austria, France, Poland, Belgium, Italy, Spain, Portugal and the US. In 1999, the company acquired the Swiss logistics company, DANZAS, and following its purchase of a minority interest of DHL International in 1998, Deutsche Post launched its partnership with DHL International, with which it was planning to align its European ground-based services.

On 20 November 2000, Deutsche Post AG made its initial public offering (IPO) on the Frankfurt Stock Exchange with the government and KfW selling some, but not all, of their holdings. Its interest in DHL International was increased to a majority in January 2002, to 75 per cent in July 2002, and to 100 per cent at the end of the year after the acquisition of the remaining shares from two investment funds and Japan Airlines.

The German government has since sold its remaining shares in Deutsche Post, now renamed Deutsche Post DHL Group, but KfW still holds a fifth of the equity and is the largest single shareholder.

Today, after five centuries of state ownership, Deutsche Post appears to have adapted well to competitive life in the private sector. It is still early days, of course, and many challenges lie ahead, but the company seems to be relatively agile, for its size (the total headcount isn't far short of half a million), and to have grasped the need for the entrepreneurial outlook, when adapting to a world in which same-day delivery, autonomous drones and ground vehicles, and AI (artificial intelligence) will be reshaping its marketplace more or less continuously.

The virtue of crises

Managers often joke that you can't save an organization that is doing well. Without discontinuities, such as mergers, survival threats, privatizations, etc., it is very hard to change organizations that are running smoothly and delivering value. This is because the output (i.e. success) validates the input (i.e. the way things are currently being done). 'If it ain't broke, don't fix it' is the common mantra. Novelty and change programmes designed to bring on change necessarily put that successful present at risk, for the sake of what programme advocates believe will be an even more successful future. There is bound to be some scepticism about this claim among the people responsible for the day-to-day running of the organization. They will cite an older, similar mantra: 'A bird in the hand is worth two in the bush.'

In the absence of an overwhelming imperative, the present has a right, even a duty, to oppose change in the same way a conventional scientific wisdom will be defended vigorously against challenge by a new paradigm. Change only occurs after conflict with, and victory over, the status quo. It must earn its place by overcoming obstacles and objections.

All organizations, however successful, must change if they are to survive and flourish, but, in resisting change, middle managers are not necessarily the villains they are usually made out to be. They often resist change for the right reasons. It is necessary to listen to and engage with them.

Middle managers resist change, because after all, it is their job to keep the organization running. If you tell them to run it differently, managers are bound to have objections not because, or not only because, they object to any change. Their intimate knowledge of how the existing system runs may enable them to see problems in a change proposal the proposers have not anticipated.

Organizations have to keep changing, in a changing world, but they must also keep running, while they are changing. As we like to say, 'the plane has to stay up in the air'. It cannot land to change or transform. Organizations need the entrepreneurial outlook for the novelty they need to adapt, but if this is allowed to disrupt or derogate the vigilance needed to keep the plane in the air, the organization will crash and burn.

Each case is unique

Major discontinuities in the development of organizations are rare opportunities to remake cultures and reset missions, but contexts of change are always multifaceted, and vary from case to case. In some cases the main adaptive pressure is financial. In other cases competitive pressures dominate and the organization's business model requires reinvention. Culture is also often a major obstacle.

In the bibliotheca case the companies chose to merge, because it seemed, to their owners, for different reasons, an advantageous stratagem. 3M wanted to divest itself of a 'non-core' business and bibliotheca's owner, OEP, wanted to widen its capabilities, and to extend its geographical reach into regions of the world neither of the two companies could have reached on its own.

They could have decided to standardize, on the culture of the acquirer, bibliotheca, and oblige the 3M culture to adapt. Instead they chose to wipe the slate clean and start again.

Deutsche Post, by contrast, had no choice. The government had granted the post office a period of transition, but with no room for any debate about the merits of privatization. Still, managers might have resisted to the point that the intransigence of the vast and crucial institution became a political issue.

The contexts of both events, the bibliotheca–3M merger and Deutsche Post's privatization were totally different, but, in both cases, the organization faced a break or discontinuity in its ordinary course of business; a gap through which emerged the entrepreneurial thinking that the enlarged bibliotheca and the new Deutsche Post had needed to adapt to their environments.

Entrepreneuring and managing

In a start-up, the entrepreneurial outlook is all you need to get an organization off the ground. It is an electric starter motor for the internal combustion engine that will drive the organization forward. It can get things going, but it is not sufficient for the long haul, when a managerial mind-set must take over.

Whenever the environment is unstable, the entrepreneurial outlook must be invoked again to realign, reset or restart the organization.

As these cases suggest, re-entrepreneuring and managing outlooks must co-exist, and ways must be found to reconcile them and ensure the tension between them is creative, rather than destructive. Although there are often tensions between the re-entrepreneuring and managing outlooks, they are far from being polar opposites. Both can coexist within the same organization and within the same individual. Even the most dyed-in-the-wool entrepreneur will readily acknowledge the value of the able management of the fruits of entrepreneurial activities. Some entrepreneurs become very able managers.

Of course, not everyone survives a re-entrepreurial transition. Just as a merger or another discontinuity such as a privatization begs questions about what to do with legacy systems, processes, and businesses that have become surplus to the new requirements, so there will be employees who cannot fit into the new world, either because of their skills or their temperament. In the case of a privatization, there may be extremely dedicated public servants, who see their resistance to the change as a matter of principle, or engineers devoted to a particular idea of quality when circumstances demand agility. Some of them will leave, but others may stay, and their scepticism will have to be managed to prevent it from subverting the transition. Some people at Deutsche Post, for example, never came to terms with ceasing to be civil servants following the IPO in 2000, and no longer working within the public service ethos. As Deutsche Post discovered, remaking a culture takes time.

A shot of entrepreneurial energy

When ideas 'get' them, entrepreneurs will move heaven and earth to realize them and will devote every waking minute to thinking about them. What in everyday life may seem like an obsession becomes, in business, a single-minded determination, or to a so-called 'serial entrepreneur', an addiction to entrepreneurial creation. Words and phrases commonly associated with entrepreneurs, such as addiction, obsession, single-minded, moving heaven and earth, and devoting every waking minute, convey a characteristic quality of entrepreneurial activity – that it is a high-energy activity, because if it was easy, it would have already been done.

Talk to entrepreneurs about their first success and most will tell you it was the most exciting time of their lives. To have an idea and turn it into a successful business, product or service is a pure act of creation that adds considerably to an entrepreneur's self-esteem, as well as, in some cases, to his or her wealth.

Something similar often happens with management buyouts. An activity deemed to be peripheral, or surplus to requirements, by the former owner can be galvanized by the entrepreneurial energy released by the deal. If the same function, with the same people, splits from its parent and becomes the core activity of an independent business, substantial amounts of latent energy and creativity are often released.

This is not only true in privatizations or buyouts. Customer support in a consultancy or an investment bank, for example, is low-status work, relative to the work of the consultants and bankers, because it is peripheral to the core business. If the same function, with the same people, splits from its parent and becomes the core activity of an independent business, substantial amounts of latent energy and creativity are often released.

As the leader of the 'buy-out team' of the publishing company mentioned at the beginning of this chapter put it: 'It was such a rush.

From being pawns in someone else's chess game, we had become major pieces in our own game.'

SUMMARY

- Disruptions in business-as-usual like mergers, acquisitions and privatizations are opportunities for re-entrepreneuring.

- Such disruptions are a good opportunity to start on a clean slate.

- Re-entrepreneuring is not a substitute for managing; both are needed, but maybe at different points of time.

- Re-entrepreneuring taps an organization's latent energy.

3

Re-structuring

New configurations, new beginnings

'What are we doing here?' 'Why are we doing it?' 'Is this where we want to be?' These are pertinent questions, no doubt. But organizations rarely indulge in that sort of introspection when business is good.

Often, only threats of closure, a takeover bid, nationalizations or privatizations can shock the company into thinking entrepreneurially again. As Samuel Johnson noted, when a man knows he is going to be hanged in a fortnight, it concentrates his mind wonderfully.

Unfortunately, managers often miss the opportunity a crisis offers. Under enormous pressure to do something, they make cost cuts that do not actually solve the problem and may even exacerbate it. Instead of taking this 'shrink to fit' approach, they would be better served by making a radical reassessment of the business model – an 'entrepreneurial restructuring'.

Entrepreneurial restructuring will still reduce costs, but its main objective goes beyond that short-term goal. The idea is not simply a quick fix, but a redesign of the business model in a way that leaves the company better adapted to its current environment.

Entrepreneurial restructuring involves making tough choices early, not simply to get through the current crisis, but to gain control over the company's future.

The first step involves finding whether the weakness is general or restricted to a part of the company. Often, particular parts of a business will still be performing well even if the overall business is troubled. Once managers have identified that healthy core, they can better focus on what they need to do next. Cost-cutting may still be in order, but finding that sustainable core ensures that the healthy business is not harmed along with the sick. Surgery is generally a better idea than bloodletting.

Ford of Europe: Restoring profitability

In 2015, Ford of Europe (FoE) leaders decided that they had to change course: In the previous five years, its European market share had fallen half a percentage point to 8 per cent. At the same time, overhead costs had risen two percentage points, leading to overall losses of about $1 billion a year. Earlier turnaround attempts had failed to deliver the results needed, but FoE leaders had no choice but to try again. This time, all options, including complete withdrawal from Europe, were on the table.

FoE was burdened by legacies of past successes. Tangible assets held the company back, including manufacturing plants in high-cost countries, such as Germany and the UK, where pension costs had been rising rapidly. Counterproductive attitudes, such as the widespread belief that large and persistent losses in Europe were somehow normal, also hindered FoE's attempts to improve the situation, particularly as many in the company did not feel vulnerable because of another erroneous belief – no matter how weak Ford sold in Europe, the company could not pull out, because FoE's engineering knowhow and skills were crucial to Ford's global success.

This time around, FoE leaders decided to try to break this complacent attitude. First, they asked corporate headquarters in Dearborn, MI, to reiterate to senior and mid-level FoE managers that 'nothing was off the table', even pulling out of Europe.

Next, they took a close look at the business and realized that the problem was not really cost, as the company had assumed, but the fact that the Ford brand and product portfolio had drifted out of sync with consumers. Overall, the brand was not clearly differentiated. Those segments where it did have relative strength were all shrinking segments.

FoE's brand positioning and differentiators are confidential, but a rough description would include such qualities as 'active' and 'sporty'. Historically, FoE had very strong motorsport credentials, in part because of its involvement with the DFV, the most successful Formula 1 racing engine of all time, which racked up 155 Grand Prix victories between 1967 and 1985.

Now FoE strategists began to look at the market, to identify which segments were being underserved by the top-selling OEMs and asked themselves first, which of these segments were being underserved by the OEMs, and second, which of these segments could Ford serve well? Based on the intersection of that Venn diagram, the team defined a target customer segment and derived from it a brand position and brand differentiators. The new plan: add new vehicles in segments with the highest growth and profit potential, such as SUVs, and eliminate less profitable lines over time.

Some veterans in senior management were uneasy about the restructuring plan. Product development people, for example, argued that the new brand positioning did not work, because it violated brand rules in a way that product development in Dearborn wouldn't allow. Other FoE leaders expected stiff resistance from unions, because the plan required taking out about 20 per cent of the cost and that inevitably meant cutting jobs.

But sceptics were won over by explanations of how the change could be implemented and the CEO's steadfast insistence that there was no alternative. The CEO and his restructuring team went to considerable lengths to get every manager involved in the turnaround project, so that no one would feel it was being imposed from above. The pushback from the unions was resolved in a similar way, through discussions rather than strikes. (3.1)

In 2015, FoE had shifted into a higher gear. By February 2016, Jim Farley, Ford's executive vice-president for Europe, Middle East and Africa, was able to point to a $259 million profit for 2015, its first in three years. 'We are creating a far more lean and efficient business that can deliver healthy returns and earn future investment,' he said.

Farley saw the improved model portfolio as a key to their success. 'When we play to our strengths, we can compete and win in Europe – even against premium brands.'

Later that year, Ford chalked up a $1.2 billion profit. In 2017, management began the next phase of the operation.

Now the company is looking ahead toward hybrid and all-electric vehicles, multi-modal transport services, and services that profit from emerging opportunities in data analytics. 'There is a huge opportunity in Europe to give our customers what they want, sometimes before they even know it, by anticipating their needs through data and data analytics,' said Roeland de Waard, Vice-President for Marketing, Sales and Service at Ford of Europe.

The Ford of Europe turnaround suggests that a successful restructuring today depends much more now on imagination than optimization. Rapid shifts in customer preferences, volatile factor prices, and disruptive competition demand that strategists take a wide-angle view of their company, its ecosystem, and its options. Whether the challenge is reinvigorating a fading brand, such as Ford of Europe, or developing a profitable niche, as we will see in the case of Zain KSA, the essential task remains the same.

Zain Saudi Arabia: Winning through caring

For the telecom Zain Saudi Arabia, restructuring also had more to do with realigning its portfolio to meet the market's need than a conventional shrink-to-fit gambit.

Theoretically, Saudi Arabia should have been a very attractive market for Zain, a Kuwait-based telecom brand with operations in seven Arab countries. The Kingdom of Saudi Arabia has the largest and wealthiest population in the region, and one of the highest technology penetration rates in the world.

But from its first year of operation, in 2007, Zain already had three major disadvantages. First, it had overpaid for the licence, $6.1 billion, more than $4 billion over the estimated fair value of $2 billion. Second, in a geographically large country, Zain's network offered significantly inferior coverage to STC, the majority state-owned incumbent and Etisalat's subsidiary Mobily, the second entrant. And third, it became clear that Zain would not enjoy the favourable regulatory environment essential for the success of a third entrant.

Saudi clients (the biggest spenders on mobile telephony in the Kingdom) quickly deserted the company, leaving it with a small customer base that consisted mostly of low-skilled expatriates.

Important suppliers became reluctant to do business with the company. To make matters even worse, Zain became embroiled in litigation with a competing operator, Mobily (Etisalat), over the fees it was paying to use Mobily's network until it could construct its own.

Burdened by all its misfortunes, Zain Saudi Arabia began to lose altitude. It kept trying and failing to expand beyond the confines of the low-value, low-skilled expatriate workers' market segment even as its cost mounted and it became more difficult to attract top telco skills and talent in the tight Saudi market. Five CEOs tried to change the direction, but all five bailed out, unable to stop its seemingly inexorable decline. It seemed simply a matter of time before the company's nosedive reached its inevitable conclusion.

When Hassan Kabbani arrived at Zain Saudi Arabia in September 2013, he recalls that he felt like a pilot who had just taken control of a plane about to crash into the ground. 'I knew that in such situations there were only two options: the first was to try to stop the plane, and the second was to accelerate, regain altitude and pass beyond the point of impact,' he said. In fact, the company had been sustaining losses of around $500 million per year, on revenues of approximately $2 billion.

In choosing the latter option, Kabbani had two convictions: 'First that the Saudi market is the most important in the region, and second that Saudis have purchasing power and want to consume data and telecommunications.' It followed from his convictions that there is room for a third operator in Saudi Arabia.

Kabbani's plan had three components:

1 Fix the basics.

2 Improve the relationship with the regulator.

3 Restructure the debt.

There were a lot of basics to be fixed. In all, Kabbani found over 250 issues that needed to be resolved. Zain needed to improve its networks, restructure its distribution, and devise what Kabbani called its 'Shabab' offer, that would position Zain as the leading mobile Internet provider in Saudi Arabia mainly for the youth segment.

As its name suggested, the 'Shabab' (youth) offer was deliberately aimed at young people. By providing unlimited access to YouTube, the 'Shabab' offer positioned Zain as the operator that gave Saudi youth their first access to streaming video. This was an important differentiator in the conservative Kingdom: there is very little public, organized entertainment in Saudi Arabia – no cinemas, and no music concerts or theatres. YouTube is the 'cinema' of choice for Saudis, and social media an important part of their social life. Mobile Internet was a lifeline for young people eager to connect with each other and to the rest of the world.

But satisfying this brand promise would not be easy, because it entailed building a 'gold standard' data network. First, Kabbani had to convince suppliers to finance the extension of the network.

'Fixing the basics' also included a new retail concept. Until 2013, Zain KSA's stores were based on the incumbents' retail model: large, colourful shops, with a wide assortment of offers. Zain simplified its offerings and chose a contrasting retail model: simple shops with well-trained staff. Kabbani chose efficiency and simplicity for its in-store experience, and invested in the professionalism of its teams, rather than in luxurious, unproductive space. This proved to be a better 'fit' than the incumbents' stores, more in keeping with contemporary value-oriented consumer preferences.

Next, he needed to build a better relationship with the regulator. Kabbani recognized that operational improvements alone would not be enough to fix the company's problems if he couldn't change its cost structure. To change that, Kabbani created a dossier of evidence demonstrating the unfair treatment that the company had received from the regulator over the years. As a direct result, the Saudi authorities issued a Royal Decree that included a 15-year extension of the company's licence, an upgrade of the licence to include fixed services, and a mandate that the Ministry of Finance negotiate with the company to assist with the latter's mounting debts. The licence extension reduced the company's amortization charge by $115 million per year for the remaining term of the licence (32 years).

The third priority was to sort out the company's finances.

Positioning Zain Saudi Arabia as the leading Internet provider and fixing the basic operational problems also had a very important side effect, the company's gross margins improved from the mid-forties when Kabbani arrived, to the mid-sixties. The Royal Decree extending the licence increased net profitability by $115 million per year.

The fact that the outcome of the two-year arbitration process to settle a $586 million claim from Mobily, ruled in Zain's favour, by awarding Mobily less than 10 per cent of its claim, made Zain's balance sheet look even healthier – a fact that did not go unnoticed by lenders.

This stronger balance sheet enabled Zain Saudi Arabia to redenominate some of its loans from Saudi riyals to US dollars to reduce the company's exposure to higher Saudi interest rates. The renewed confidence in the company from investors and lenders also reduced Zain's cost of capital to normal levels.

Kabbani's plan, which he called 'Winning through Caring', worked. In 2013, Zain KSA had 7 million, relatively low-value customers. By 2017 it had more than 10 million customers and gross earnings had risen to double the 2013 figure. Best of all, the company posted its first quarterly net profit since it entered the market 9 years earlier.

Kabbani attributes the turnaround's success to three factors:

1 Taking the time to identify the real problems.

2 Aligning the company's product mix with market demand, specifically deciding to become the operator for young people.

3 Developing a good plan with a team that understood their roles.

In other words, creative re-entrepreneuring – repositioning existing assets in a new way – had saved the company when it might easily have failed. Many other companies have succeeded in similar ways. As we shall see in the next case, SMA, a German solar firm that was being undercut by Chinese competitors, also found its salvation by redefining the terms of competition.

SMA Solar Technology: The sun will come out tomorrow

'If we want things to stay as they are, things will have to change' . . . This famous line from Giuseppe Tomasi di Lampedusa's novel *The Leopard* could have been pronounced by the leaders of SMA Solar Technology, the world's largest maker of solar inverters, when the crisis in the solar industry hit.

After a booming start on the German market, the sector got caught between two trends in the late 2000s: on the one hand, falling prices brought on by Chinese competition. On the other hand, the German government, seeing that the global solar market was adding solar power capacity at a rapid pace, decided the market no longer needed the same level of subsidy.

As a producer of solar inverters for photovoltaics systems, SMA was long protected from the crisis, as the production of inverters requires deeper technological competence than that of panels or cells. While several major panel manufacturers such as Q-Cells, Solarhybrid, Solar Millennium and Solon went bankrupt as Chinese firms began to flood the market with low-cost panels (3.2), SMA's rapid revenue growth continued. It reached a peak of €2 billion in 2010.

But price pressure soon affected inverters and, in the early 2010s, the company found itself locked in a constant revenue decline across almost all of its business lines. SMA had grown quickly, in the context of the solar boom, in order to serve an increasing demand. Overhead costs could not be reduced as fast as needed, causing a severe earnings crisis and cash burn. In November 2014, management announced that it had to resize the cost structure, as the bottom line was hit by weak demand for its products.

SMA had to react, and decided to implement a comprehensive restructuring programme, targeting both personnel and operating costs. No functional areas were exempt: Technology, operations, sales, services and administration all faced deep cuts, with an objective of reducing the break-even from a revenue level of €1 billion to €700 million. The programme was smoothly implemented – personnel reductions were fully achieved by a voluntary programme – and, most importantly, quickly successful. Fixed costs were reduced by 40 per cent by the end of the first year (3.3). Managers credited their success to a comprehensive communication, and the inclusion of the workers' council from the beginning of the effort. Including the workers early on helped to ensure that the entire organization shared a common view of the challenge and its solution.

This could look like a classic restructuring case. But it was more than that. For even as they shrank the company to fit the new economic reality, executives redesigned the way the company developed its products. SMA had to achieve a feat: reducing its cost base while remaining a tech leader in a fast-moving industry. The question was: how to deliver R&D activities with half the staff, and without losing the knowledge and technical excellence that were key to the future of the group? This is why the firm re-organized its R&D department.

SMA executives decided to move from a product-centric approach to a solution-providing philosophy. A technology centre was set up, functioning as a platform for pooling research resources between string and central inverter units. Organizers intended the development centre to serve as the heart of the new consolidated R&D programme, and designed it along four project-related work streams: software, layout, mechanics and power-electronics.

To maintain the group's capacity for innovation, while allocating resources in a more efficient way, SMA decided to commoditize its flagship product, the inverter, and to place added value in offering integrated solutions, tailored to different needs. Today, the manufacturing of the product no longer drives the design of solutions. Instead, customer demand and market segmentation becomes the starting point. The basic product is now 80 per cent standardized worldwide, then customized and differentiated according to the technical specifications required by the local market. This mental and organizational revolution was successful: the significant reduction of cost and headcount (to 50 per cent in R&D) only had a minor impact on the output, due to a huge efficiency gain.

The overall restructuring process enabled the company to return to profitability and recover its stock price. The recovery of the group as a whole, whose stock price was multiplied by four in a year, was spectacular. The storm is over, and SMA is now a strong champion on the solar market. Thanks to its re-entrepreneuring instincts, the company found a way to compete in a new ecosystem even as many of its peers expired.

Other times, as we will see in the next case, the challenge is less about adapting to a changed environment than accepting that the original vision had overlooked some crucial variables. In such a case, the secret ingredient is the courage to accept the fact that the original plan has failed, and that the only way forward is by way of a humbler path.

bauMax: Error correction

In 2012, bauMax, an Austrian do-it-yourself retailer, suddenly found it had a massive remodelling project on its hands. Spread out across nine Central and Eastern European (CEE) countries, the chain ran into a sudden earnings and liquidity crisis.

Managers' first response was to tighten the chain's inventory. This didn't solve the liquidity problem, but it bought the company more time. Fortunately, they were able to manage their stock so well that the business kept going for two weeks after its bankers temporarily froze all of bauMax's credit lines. As a team member said: 'It was like flying a jumbo jet without fuel.'

In retrospect, it is clear that the main problem at bauMax was the collision of two factors: excessive entrepreneurial optimism and the 2008 financial crisis.

bauMax's founder, Karlheinz Essl Sr., had had considerable success in his 'core' markets of Austria, the Czech Republic, and Slovakia in the 1990s, and in the early 2000s, began to expand to other Central European markets, at a time when demand was buoyant and most businesses were expanding.

But Essl and his team had a blind spot: although demand was buoyant everywhere, per capita income and purchasing power varied significantly between markets. Rather than tailoring their inventory and footprint to suit the local market, they built the same large stores that had been successful in Austria, the Czech Republic and Slovakia, in the countries the company expanded to – Slovenia, Hungary, Romania, Bulgaria, Croatia and Turkey – where purchasing power was considerably lower.

After the dust of the financial crisis had settled, bauMax was left with its old profitable core businesses in Austria, the Czech Republic and Slovakia, but overextended in regions that were suffering deep economic difficulties.

However, the company could not just walk away. It held long-term leases on troubled stores that required substantial, continual investments in inventory to keep the losses from being even worse. Nor could bauMax walk away without incurring substantial exit costs. As a member of the team put it, 'There was this slow creeping death from the periphery, coming ever closer to the core.'

But bauMax managers had a plan: Many of their stores were in good locations and had the potential to become healthy businesses. If they were to be saved, they had to persuade their landlords and the banks to hold their fire. If they agreed on rent reductions at the potentially viable outlets and debt rescheduling for the group overall, the potentially profitable stores could be sold as going concerns.

It was a complex and time-consuming process, because the team had to negotiate with conflicting interests and find common ground with creditors, potential buyers and, most of all, suppliers, who had to keep the stores stocked while this was going on. An additional complicating factor was extensive media coverage of the affair in all countries affected. This created uncertainty, because customers and suppliers sometimes got the news about the latest wrinkles in the crisis before executives made an official announcement. A lot of effort had to be made to calm the nerves of employees, creditors and suppliers.

Unlikely as it might have sometimes seemed, common ground was found. Creditors understood the threat of a messy insolvency and agreed to the proposed restructuring in the belief that it would produce the least-worst outcome.

The restructuring plan proposed breaking bauMax into three entities:

1 OpCo, the operations company;

2 PropCo, bauMax's real estate assets, which would be sold to a real estate investor;

3 BadMax, where executives gathered everything investors would not want, including unprofitable stores and unprofitable contracts, 'all the things which are not tenable', as someone close to the developments put it.

The assets of OpCo and PropCo were sold to retailers and real-estate investors respectively, while BadMax was given enough money to wind down gracefully. Of the nine country operations, only two were liquidated. The rest were sold to DIY chains, or to other kinds of retailers.

The OpCo and PropCo relationships were far from straightforward to negotiate. The value of the real estate would be affected by the rental agreement with the resident store, which would affect the value of the store to retail buyers. Charge more rent, and bauMax would get a higher price for the property, but a lower price for the stores, and vice versa. These trade-offs had to be agreed between OpCo and PropCo buyers in advance before either transaction could be completed.

In the end, the employees, apart from those at the headquarters, kept their jobs. All suppliers were paid in full, and even the banks that had financed the company's expansion recovered nearly 64 per cent of their investment.

Looking back, the restructuring team attributes the success of the project, the largest restructuring ever undertaken in Central and Eastern Europe in terms of debt volume and sales, to the trust bauMax managers had established between all the interested parties. It was a large and very complicated undertaking, full of uncertainties, which could have been derailed at any time by an insistent bank, an impatient supplier, or an adamant buyer.

RESTRUCTURING WITH AN ENTREPRENEURIAL EYE

AS THESE TWO CASES SUGGEST, an 'entrepreneurial' restructuring puts an adapted business model at the heart of the project. It takes nothing for granted and even contemplates closure of the business. It asks such basic questions as: 'If this business didn't exist, would it be an entrepreneurial opportunity today?'

The adapted business model that leaders develop differs from business to business, but all companies that have a successful entrepreneurial restructuring tend to do many of the same things. In particular, they

1   *Develop intelligence systems.* They establish and then maintain an accurate and sensitive intelligence gathering system with the extended reach entrepreneurs need, to spot opportunities, threats and resources beyond the company, the country or the industry.

2 *See the worst case, as the real case.* They plan for the worst, and contemplate closure or withdrawal, but strive for the new and the best.

3 *Do with, not to.* They listen to employees and their ideas. They get them used to contributing. Mobilize, motivate and empower them.

4 *Speak as openly as they can about how things are going.* They make the whole restructuring process as open as practicable, by establishing good internal and external communication systems.

5 *Get the decision-makers on board.* Anyone with decision-making responsibilities who has an interest in the restructuring has the power to frustrate and to facilitate it. They make sure that stakeholders are carefully managed.

6 *Give key employees and stakeholders incentives.* They offer key people incentives to commit themselves and contribute ideas to the programme.

7 *Create a dashboard.* They establish a simple, understandable system for monitoring progress.

8 *Look for real change.* They don't tick boxes: instead, they seek out real, measurable, improvements in all the relevant areas. Experiment, and analyse the results.

9 *Embody the change.* They lead by example and appoint ambassadors to spread the word.

10 *Make performance an attitude.* They create a performance culture by adapting organizational structures and accountabilities.

Entrepreneurial restructuring always takes care of first things first. It deals with the big issues in the beginning, and only turns to cost measures once such big issues have been settled.

No exit

As the bauMax case suggests, a company's strategic plan is always in danger of drifting out of sync with its environment. The leaders of bauMax were fortunate enough to correct the company's course in time, but companies are often not so lucky. A better approach is to review where you are and where you are going again and again. Each sector has its own rhythm, and those rhythms may change over time. The faster the sectoral rhythms, the more frequently restructurings must be made, and the stronger the case for 're-entrepreneuring'.

But as we will see with the Ruhrkohle case, not every problem has a solution. Sometimes, managers must accept the fact that the world has changed, and mitigate the damage of the company's inevitable end as best they can. In the case of Ruhrkohle AG, one of Germany's last great coal companies, smart planning could not save the company, but it did minimize the pain to its stakeholders and protected future generations from environmental harm.

Ruhrkohle: A painless death

Ruhrkohle AG, an agglomeration of dozens of local mining companies brought together in the 1970s, employed over 150,000 miners in the Rhein/Ruhr region at the turn of the millennium. In 2000, Ruhrkohle was Germany's largest coal producer, operating over 100 mines, but its size was no help. In the early 1990s, the company faced two mortal threats: pressure from the European Union to phase out subsidies, and the impossibility of competing with much lower-cost foreign producers if those subsidies were eliminated. Since the coal market had globalized in the early 1990s and China had emerged as a major low-cost exporter, the future for expensive, deep-mined German coal had begun to look uncertain.

The government faced a stark choice: either continue to hand out subsidies to mining companies, including Ruhrkohle, at an accelerating rate as global coal prices fell to keep miners in work, or withdraw subsidies and spend more money on the workers' retirement and unemployment. When the government decided to do the latter, the writing was on the wall for Ruhrkohle. All Ruhrkohle executives could do was organize and manage an orderly closure that inflicted as little pain as possible on the employees and other key stakeholders. (3.4)

In the 1990s, a long-term plan was drafted to manage a phased decline and ultimate dissolution. In addition to phased capacity cuts, asset sales, reorganization and long-term risk management, the plan covered what Ruhrkohle saw as its substantial social responsibilities. Working together, the three key parties – Ruhrkohle, the government, and the unions – reached an understanding. Over a long series of discussions, they devised a long-term wind-down: a 20+-year timeline, at the end of which a very large and historic enterprise would be reduced to a memory, without causing any significant social or economic problems.

Twenty years later, the first phase of the plan is complete. Ruhrkohle's last mine is scheduled to close down in 2018. In the coming months, the employee register should fall to zero. That might sound like a failure, but if we define a company as an enterprise that meets its commitments to its stakeholders, Ruhrkohle was actually a success:

First, none of Ruhrkohle's employees became unemployed as a consequence of the phased dissolution of the company. All miners and other employees either obtained jobs in other industries after receiving free education or retraining, or took early retirement at 48. These benefits were, of course, another form of government subsidy, but much cheaper and more compliant with the EU's proscription of state subsidies, which would be less expensive for the government and less distorting for the German economy than continuing to make good Ruhrkohle's mounting losses. What might have been an economic and social catastrophe was handled instead rather painlessly.

Second, the unions also helped make the first phase of the shutdown a success. IG Bergbau, Chemie, Energie, the union representing Ruhrkohle employees, could see the writing on the wall, too. The unions fought hard for their members' rights, but didn't follow the example of the UK's National Union of Mineworkers in the 1980s, and try to prevent pit closures. The German miners' union became part of the solution, rather than the problem unions have often been in other countries, when faced with the same existential threat. No layoffs, strikes, or social conflicts served to magnify the crisis.

But the longest phase of the shutdown has barely begun. For centuries to come, a foundation funded through asset sales will keep the mines from contaminating the region. These costs will be substantial, because when a deep mine (some of Ruhrkohle's mines were as much as a kilometre deep) is closed, it fills with ground water. If this is not pumped out, the ground above can collapse many years later, by which time houses or factories may have been built on it. This perpetual risk is being managed by Ruhrkohle Stiftung, a foundation with an endowment of €3 billion from Ruhrkohle asset sales, a sizeable portfolio expected to be sufficient to keep the mines dry for centuries.

The lesson of the Ruhrkohle story is that although re-entrepreneuring always takes courage, sometimes, it is the courage to acknowledge that the company's time has passed, and then find a way for the organization to wind up its social and financial obligations in a responsible way.

The Ruhrkohle story might seem like an extreme case but, given the growing speed of technological change, it is one that more companies are likely to face in the coming years. As sectoral rhythms speed up, restructurings are likely to become more frequent, and the need for re-entrepreneuring more acute.

Taking an entrepreneurial approach to restructuring early should help you avoid the necessity of a complete wind-down. In any case, acting on a clear-sighted view of the company's situation is more likely to lead to a more positive outcome for the company and its stakeholders than an outdated view of the firm's position.

SUMMARY

- Entrepreneurial restructuring turns a near-death experience into an opportunity for entrepreneurialism.
- The way to begin is to look for a healthy core.
- The more volatile the environment, the more often entrepreneurial restructuring is required.
- Sometimes, the right answer to the question, 'what next?', is to face reality and shut down operations.

4

Re-form

Re-entrepreneuring in non-entrepreneurial contexts

A sprawling rail network that spans 11 time zones. More than a century of state ownership. Steadily falling passenger volumes in the face of new competition. Most businesses today operate in a complex environment, but the Russian Railways faced a challenge of another order of magnitude: Was this old institution ready to adapt to a new era of mobility?

As tough as it can be to drive change in a company, the managers of state-owned enterprises and government agencies – such as Russian Railways – generally have it even tougher. The public sector operates with a completely different set of dynamics, whether it is in terms of culture and ethos, or processes and practices. Conventional solutions that are easy to deploy in the private sector might not always find favour in the public sector.

This chapter looks at a number of cases where a small group of insightful individuals overcame long odds within enormous institutions to create dramatic sustainable change. From a new venture for the world's largest railroad system to the fast-paced privatization of the former East Germany and the passage of Germany's transformative Hartz labour reforms, the secret of their success is smart re-entrepreneuring.

Of course, any successful re-entrepreneuring initiative, whether in the public or the private sector, depends on leaders with entrepreneurial attitudes. This may be even more true within governmental institutions. What does it take to succeed despite such overwhelming inertia? To find out, we asked Amitabh Kant, an Indian civil servant who has managed to make substantive changes within the Indian government, one of the world's most notoriously intractable bureaucracies.

Russian Railways: From platforms to 'platform'

As with many formerly Soviet institutions, Russian Railways has had a bumpy transition toward its identity as a private sector company. Thanks in part to the growing popularity of air travel in the world's largest country, the outlook for FPC, the passenger division of Russian Railways, did not look good.

A traditional restructuring approach was not an option: it would have meant managing a long decline in the face of faster and more convenient modes of transportation, trying and failing year after year to staunch falling numbers on many of its routes, even the iconic Trans-Siberian Railway. Instead, FPC needed a new opportunity – and found it, in a phenomenon that looked at first like a threat.

On the competitive periphery of FPC's business, new online ticket sellers had started popping up, digital travel portals and smartphone apps that sought to become intermediaries between passengers and operators. In Russia, as in most markets, travellers now wanted integrated, easy-to-use travel solutions, all-in-one portals that made it easy to combine rail transport with auto rentals, and ride-sharing platforms.

But none of them had succeeded in introducing a completely integrated online travel service to the Russian market. Most transportation operators and online travel portals still offered only 'station-to-station' options that lacked multi-modal capability. This represented a risk for FPC: if someone else filled this multi-modal gap, FPC risked losing its traditional connection with the customer. On the other hand, if it found a way to move fast enough, this opening could also represent an opportunity to maintain its connection even as the Russian travellers' relationship to trains evolved.

The leaders of FPC had long watched other modes of travel whittle away at their revenues without much possibility of recourse. Here was a threat, however, that they could do something about: they held an ace in this particular game because although its passenger service was declining, FPC still maintained one of the country's largest databases of transportation customers.

Before FPC's portal team began building the platform, they looked at the recent innovative platforms like Rome2Rio, Moovit and Trafi, and at the solutions of traditional players, such as Deutsche Bahn, SNCF and Daimler.

Based on their research, FPC strategists decided they had an opportunity to go further than any Western European travel portal had dared, and create a completely integrated offer embracing all transport modes for the whole country, accessible with a 'one-click' payment. The solution would have to meet three key customer needs in a way that the best of the western sites already did:

- user-friendly trip management with a single interface;
- shorter journey times via selection of optimal routes;
- clearly calculated door-to-door trip cost.

At the same time, the new platform would also offer benefits for the train and other transportation providers, by offering options that the traveller might not have previously considered based on FPC's better knowledge of customers and their needs, and going beyond transportation offerings. Done right, FPC's service could even become a prototype of a global transportation agency, a kind of booking.com for multi-modal transport.

FPC managers realized they needed three things to achieve a successful launch: user-friendly technology, the ability to test the model on a large scale, and speed and flexibility both in product adaptation and decision-making. The third success factor – speed and flexibility – was the main challenge for the railway.

To speed up development, the company brought in a technical partner as a co-investor. This partner would deliver new capabilities and competencies and, on top of that, offer a Silicon Valley-style approach to management. The management structure would be flatter at the new entity, on the theory that fewer layers of reporting should reduce the time from decision-making to execution.

Will they succeed? So far, the signs are promising. The new company has launched a business-to-business solution for selling rail tickets with its co-investing technology partner, and is testing the new consumer website that will feature door-to-door travel planning.

Even though it is still early days for FPC, the experiment shows that, if harnessed well, the power of re-entrepreneuring can be truly awe-inspiring. Occasionally, it has been able to transform not just an enterprise but an entire country. Under the stewardship of Lee Kuan Yew, for example, Singapore went from being one of the world's poorest countries, with a per capita GDP of $516 a year in 1965, to one of the richest, with per capita GDP of more than $53,000. The People's Republic of China has made similarly spectacular gains, arguably through a similar process, transforming itself in just three decades from a country with serious difficulties even feeding itself to a world leader in many industries, including genetics, artificial intelligence and solar energy. As we shall see in the next case, the privatization of former state-owned assets in reunified Germany, intelligent management can create value with re-entrepreneuring regardless of the culture, political system, or source of capital.

Treuhandanstalt: Reviving East Germany's corporate sector

Formal reunification of East and West Germany occurred on 3 October 1990, following a year of discussions and negotiations on how to realize the monetary, economic and social union. An important milestone during the run-up to reunification was the formation of the Treuhandanstalt (THA – literally, 'trust agency') in July 1990. Its particular mission: privatize the economy by re-entrepreneuring the assets of the former German Democratic Republic.

The THA's portfolio included 2.4 million hectares of forest, agricultural and commercial land, and the assets of state agencies, such as the Stasi (the State Security Service or Staatssicherheitsdienst, East Germany's secret police) and the National People's Army, and 12,500 state-owned enterprises (SOEs). The Treuhand companies alone employed a total of 4 million people, a quarter of the East German population.

It was an enormous task but speed was essential, given the inability of many of the SOEs to compete without the protection of trade within East Germany and other Warsaw Pact countries. If they continued to try to hawk shoddy goods on the open market, most companies would soon fail if they were not quickly restructured into viable businesses. There was no choice for a longer process. With the decision for a single currency already in place, global competition was a reality.

Over the next few years, the THA restructured and then privatized most of the enterprises, raising DEM 60 billion for the new reunified government. As THA President Birgit Breuel noted in the mid-1990s, in just 'four-and-a-half years, an entire economy has been transformed and, in large part, is now competitive'.

Part of the success was due to the unusual governance structure of the THA. A management committee, which reported to the THA, served as an independent review board and an 'initiator and engine' of the transformation.

The committee completed descriptions and analysis of all the enterprises under the THA's mandate in just four weeks. At the same time, committee analysts reviewed 2,000 restructuring and business plans. Each business was placed in one of six categories with different recommendations for disposal, and submitted to the THA for approval. Separate analyses of some 200 'cash-gobbling' organizations that required immediate attention were also undertaken to establish their short- and medium-term funding requirements, and to identify restructuring opportunities.

Fielding requests from THA portfolio companies for liquidity support was an early duty of the committee. The committee considered about 1,000 such requests for liquidity support from THA companies and granted DEM 28 billion worth of secured loans to bridge the short-term cash needs of their portfolio companies.

The agency adopted an eclectic approach to privatization that included both conventional vehicles and innovative organizational forms such as limited partnerships. The THA committee also stood ready to mediate in deadlocked, or particularly tricky privatization negotiations, and actively supported restructuring.

Every restructuring plan had to comply with two sets of guidelines before the THA would extend financing to the operator. The first set of guidelines covered the legal status, company structure, management, product range, main customers, plants and offices, production facilities, employees, delivery obligations in Comecon countries, risks from contaminated sites, and the type and number of co-operative relationships of the old SoEs. The second set of guidelines was more forward-looking. It addressed the organization's product and operations strategy (also compared to those of its West German and international competitors), its human resources strategy and its integrated business plan, including any restructuring actions.

THA officials estimated that only 2 per cent of firms needed no restructuring. Around two-thirds could be restructured, and 21 per cent needed to be closed.

Broadly speaking, industries with business customers (B2B) tended to be in better shape than consumer goods companies, and small- and medium-sized enterprises (SMEs, companies with up to 1,000 employees, Germany's strong suit in terms of size), had a higher proportion of promising candidates than large firms. To some, the enduring strength of the GDR's SMEs (*Mittelstand*) suggested that entrepreneurialism had not been completely eradicated in the GDR, but was merely dormant and now awaited only a change in the environment to demonstrate its power.

Generally speaking, the larger organizations tended to be more challenging, but there were some successes. The re-entrepreneuring of Kombinat VEB Carl Zeiss Jena from a sleepy East German optical equipment company into a world leader in laser optics may have been the most impressive resurrection of a large company.

VEB Carl Zeiss Jena was created after World War 2 out of the expropriated East German subsidiary of Carl Zeiss. It consisted of all 25 enterprises in East Germany's optical equipment industry. At the time of its transfer to the THA, the company employed 69,000 people.

VEB Carl Zeiss Jena was well known for producing high-quality products. Some analysts believed it to be one of the few East German firms that could potentially compete on a global basis, but they later learned that only certain units had that potential. After reunification, the THA took over VEB Carl Zeiss Jena and carved out Jenoptik, divesting other resources as Carl Zeiss Jena GmbH into the West German lens maker now known as Carl Zeiss AG and located in the town of Oberkochen.

In its first financial year, Carl Zeiss Jena GmbH missed its sales forecast by nearly 50 per cent – instead of the planned DEM

200 million, sales reached DEM 101 million – and lost investors a total of DEM 146 million. In its second financial year, Zeiss missed another set of business forecasts. Four hundred people were laid off and the microscopy business relocated from Jena to Oberkochen, reuniting the old pre-war Zeiss group. Further restructurings followed within Carl Zeiss AG, led by CEO Peter Grassmann, the former head of Siemens healthcare division. By 1999–2000, Carl Zeiss Jena GmbH turned the corner and became profitable once more.

The other part of VEB Carl Zeiss Jena, Jenoptik, took a similar path of restructuring and re-entrepreneuring. In June 1991, Lothar Späth, the former Prime Minister of Baden-Wurttemberg, became the CEO of Jenoptik. Specializing in the areas of photonics, optoelectronics and mechatronics, it remained for a time under ownership by the state government of Thuringia. Späth tried to give his entrepreneurial spirit to Jenoptik, selling units he thought weakened the company and then reinvesting in more promising assets, and shedding staff. During the restructuring process, 50,000 people lost their jobs. In 1994, Jenoptik purchased Meissner + Wurst, a company specialized in building laboratories and production plants for high-tech applications. Jenoptik became an AG in 1996, and in 1998 the company was strong enough to be listed on the Frankfurt Stock Exchange. Since the flotation, Jenoptik has grown substantially and expanded internationally. Today, the company operates in more than 80 countries and maintains production facilities in Germany, France, Switzerland and the US. It is now the global leader for diode lasers. Revenues reached €684.8 million in 2016, EBITDA was €96.9 million, and a lean staff of 3,600. (4.1)

Another group was disposed of through management buy-outs (MBOs). A total of 3,000 'Treuhand companies' privatized through

MBOs. Such management-led privatizations accounted for about 22 per cent of the total number of Treuhand-reformed companies, but because they were mostly SMEs, they accounted for only about 5 per cent of the former GDR's productive assets.

The Treuhand MBOs compressed about 50 years of industrial development into just a few years. At the start of the process, the company's average headcount stood at 106 employees. By June 1994, the figure had dropped to 28. Experts consider the THA's MBOs to have been a success. 'In nearly a quarter of the MBO firms, profits are better than expected and approximately every sixth MBO has already started to increase the number of employees they had previously cut,' wrote THA's chroniclers Dieter Bös and Gunter Kayser – another illustration of the 'reculer, pour mieux sauter' principle we noted in Chapter 1.

German labour market reform

In the early 1990s, Germany had one of Europe's weaker economies. Germany had the highest rate of unemployment in the European Union, after Spain, including a growing proportion of structural unemployment, as the former GDR's organizations hurriedly adapted to competitive market conditions. (As noted above, the average headcount at former GDR SMEs had fallen from 106 to 28 by 1994.) Thanks partly to the high cost of reunification, the federal government as well as the old West German federal states were struggling with growing indebtedness, and rates of investment were unusually low. The rate of gross fixed capital formation fell by 3.4 per cent a year between 2000 and 2004, private and state consumption was muted compared to those of other industrialized countries, such as the UK and the US, and in the early 2000s Germany's net rate of investment was the lowest in the entire OECD.

Other German weaknesses included a relatively inefficient tax system and inflexible labour markets. Average German labour costs were €27.1 an hour, compared to €20.2 in France, €19.9 in the US and €18.7 in the UK. Overall, a united Germany recorded an average growth rate of only 1.5 per cent a year between 1991 and 2002, a full percentage point below the OECD average. In purchasing power parity (PPP) terms, Germany's GDP per capita ranking among European Union countries fell from 4th in 1994 to 11th in 2004.

In short, Germany's international competitiveness and economic growth were falling and costs and indebtedness were rising. It was clear to many Germans, including Gerhard Schröder the new Chancellor, that something had to be done. Schröder began with tax reform, which passed in 2000, and then continued with a new proposal, Agenda 2010 – a comprehensive package of reforms in the fields of pensions, health and labour. To work out the details, Schröder deputized a panel of 15 business, academic and political leaders, the Committee for Modern Services in the Labour Market. Chaired by Volkswagen's director of Human Resources, Peter Hartz, the 'Hartz committee' included employers, politicians, unions and research institutes who were charged with making recommendations for the reform of the German labour market.

To prepare the reform by such a committee was extraordinary. Although German business and labour are normally less adversarial than in some European countries, normally only the Ministry for Economy and Labour would have been involved in drafting new labour laws. Having a broad, plural base enabled Schröder to bypass the typical negotiation processes in political parties and shorten the parliamentary discussions. (4.2)

The four so-called 'Hartz reforms', designed to make Germany's labour market more flexible, became law between January 2003 and January 2006. The main changes were:

- the period unemployment benefit I (Arbeitslosengeld I) was to be paid was substantially reduced;[1]

- unemployment benefit and social care were merged, to become Arbeitslosengeld II, and its rate was reduced to, or below, the level of the former social care;

- stricter criteria for accepting job offers and the introduction of sanctions if job offers are refused;

- reform and restructuring of job agencies;

- support for subcontracted work;

- support of 'Me plcs' in the form of a business start-up grant to promote self-employment among the unemployed;

- adaptations in the field of mini- and midi-jobs.

After the enactment of the Hartz reforms, reductions in the non-wage costs of employment, such as unemployment benefit and unemployment insurance rates (from 6.5 per cent in 2003 to 3.0 per cent in 2013) have reduced total employment costs substantially. At 28 per cent of total wage costs in 2015 (compared with 44 per cent before the Hartz reforms), the share of non-wage costs in total German employment costs was lower in Germany than the EU and Eurozone averages. As a result, German unemployment fell steadily, from 11.7 per cent in 2003 to 6.1 per cent in 2016. Today, Germany's unemployment rate is only 3.6 per cent,[2] less than half the European average.

Entrepreneurs everywhere

Finally, it is worth keeping in mind that as with any kind of re-entrepreneuring project, entrepreneurial action in the public sector depends in no small part on the effectiveness of the entrepreneur behind it.

The good news is that not only do such people exist, but occasionally they succeed. Anyone who assumes that entrepreneurialism is too fragile a flower to blossom under state bureaucracy should consider the career of the Indian government administrator Amitabh Kant, who is currently the CEO of NITI Aayog (NITI is short for National Institution for Transforming India. It is also a backronym: in Hindi, 'niti' is the word for policy).

A 2012 study by the Hong Kong-based Political and Economic Risk Consultancy rated Indian bureaucracy as the worst in Asia. Yet despite having to work in what is generally regarded as an incompetent, inefficient and unproductive system, Kant has still managed to drive real change for the country.

Among other distinctions, Kant is the mastermind of the 'Make in India' initiative, which aims to change India into a manufacturing hub. Since its launch in 2014, Make in India has worked to improve the ease of doing business in India and has attracted companies to manufacture or do R&D in India, companies like Huawei, Mercedes-Benz, Hyundai, Foxconn, Xiaomi, Schneider Electric, Sony, Lenovo and Motorola.

He was also behind the hugely successful 'Incredible India', and 'God's Own Country' campaigns that promoted India and Kerala State respectively as destinations for manufacturing and tourism. These campaigns won several international awards, and included such activities as infrastructure development and public–private partnerships, as well as more conventional positioning and branding. Previously neglected by tourists, Kerala State subsequently became one of India's leading tourism destinations.

Today, Kant is continuing his work, now as head of NITI Aayog, a think-tank that is working to introduce a results-driven mind-set in India's government sector, which tends to be mired in a thicket of regulations and bureaucratic thinking. As Kant puts it, 'We have tried to make NITI Aayog as private sector-oriented in its decision-making process as feasible.'

How has he overcome the deep lethargy of India's slow-moving, silo-bound bureaucracy, despite such long odds? It seems to come down to two habits of thought. The first is to focus on the advantages of public enterprise:

- It has a clearly defined constituency that it knows well.
- In most democracies its institutions are seen as relatively trustworthy.
- It derives considerable entrepreneurial energy from its strong public service ethos.
- It has substantial borrowing and buying power.
- It has a tradition of successful partnerships.

The second, to follow five best practices:

KANT'S RULES OF BUREAUCRATIC RE-ENTREPRENEURING

- Real time data-driven decision-making and outcome-based monitoring is essential.

- Policymakers should make extensive use of current technology to streamline the citizen–government interface and be informed on potential future technological transformations.

- Government leaders should make an effort to drive behavioural change in their organizations by creating an environment where new ideas are given room and the work culture is open and outcome-based.

- Government leaders should articulate a grand vision and do-able mission. Bold decision-making should be encouraged. Government leaders should be able to quickly understand the big picture so that they can visualize the true pros and cons of every decision they make.

- A competitive environment should be created between states and stakeholders while keeping outcome delivery the keystone of all efforts.

In the end, re-entrepreneuring any kind of organization involves going back to the basics, both with respect to the meaning of the organization and instilling a sense of purpose in the people who work for it. This may be even truer within a governmental agency, where executives seldom have pay-related incentives at their disposal. As Mike Duggan, mayor of Detroit and the leader of a remarkable recent turnaround has noted, 'People get into public service because something in their heart wants them to help people, and over time the bureaucracy beats that idealism out of them. We are trying to bring [idealism] back.'

But as in the private sector, public sector re-entrepreneuring is in part a matter of getting every employee to share a larger vision and then act on that vision. As Duggan puts it,

> If each individual person says, OK my job is to get the grass cut in the parks; my job is to get the tractors repaired 20 per cent faster [to get] the grass cut in the parks ... turnaround occurs. Not because one or two leaders do some brilliant thing – turnaround occurs when everybody in the organization performs better.
>
> (4.3)

SUMMARY

- Private or public sector, re-entrepreneuring an organization depends on entrepreneurial leadership.

- The leader must have a bold vision for the future and be ready to act on that vision.

- At the same time, be clear about current shortcomings. You can't reform an organization if you haven't first defined the problem.

- It's the system, stupid: in a dysfunctional organization, you can only drive real change if you change the culture.

5

Re-conceiving

Finding value beyond the core

Usually, re-entrepreneuring involves looking at an existing set of assets in a new way. Some of the time, however, it entails looking at an entirely new part of the value chain – or a new industry altogether.

Conventional organizations often take their positions on the value chain for granted. Entrepreneurial organizations look at the value chain as a whole and see opportunities where most might see blockages, weaknesses and other imperfections. Not wedded to particular niches, they are ready to migrate up – or down and even beyond – the value chain to wherever they see the most promising opportunities.

In this chapter, we review the cases of three companies that faced their growth challenge by making just such a radical redefinition of their role.

To infinity and beyond!

Pixar's dramatic metamorphosis from hardware producer to digital animator shows just how many possibilities can open up once you adjust your opportunity viewfinder.

When Steve Jobs bought a 70 per cent interest in *Star Wars* filmmaker Lucasfilm's computer division in 1986, soon after his resignation from Apple, the main attraction was the Pixar Image Computer, from which the new standalone company part-owned by its employees took its name. The Pixar machine sold for $125,000. It was a high-end machine marketed to graphic designers and animators to render three-dimensional objects; to medical imaging specialists to render 3D CAT scans; and to military analysts to render images from satellites and reconnaissance flights.

Jobs liked two things about the business. First, Pixar's hardware was designed around its software, particularly its REYES rendering program (for 'Renders Everything You Ever Saw'). Jobs preferred computers with a high degree of hardware/software integration – that had been a key ingredient in Apple's secret sauce. Second, the computer straddled the border between technology and art, a frontier where most technologists and artists alike feel uncomfortable, but where Jobs felt in his element.

Initially, Jobs wanted to expand Pixar's markets by producing cheaper, cut-down versions of the image computer and the REYES rendering program. However, his new colleagues were not enthusiastic and he dropped the idea.

The business struggled, but it did establish one important new relationship: when Roy Disney, Walt's nephew, wanted to reanimate

Disney's animation unit, he asked Pixar to help. Pixar developed a suite of animation tools for Disney, which animators first used in 1988 in *The Little Mermaid*. The retelling of the Hans Christian Andersen tale went on to be the company's first commercially successful animated film in decades and a huge box-office hit.

In Pixar's original incarnation as a computing company, management had seen the digital animation division as a showcase for their computer system, but as luck would have it, this division was led by John Lasseter, a gifted, visionary animator with whom Jobs forged a strong bond. Jobs was delighted when Lasseter's animated short film, *Luxo Jr*, starring a parent and child represented as desk lamps, won the best film award at an annual computer graphics conference in 1986. Jobs saw promise in Lasseter and his team. Even as most of Pixar languished, he protected Lasseter from cost cuts and agreed to finance another short film, *Tin Toy*, which, in 1988, became the first computer-generated film to win an Academy Award. (*Tin Toy* later became the inspiration for the blockbuster *Toy Story*.)

Jobs slid easily from the technology value chain to the entertainment value chain. As Lasseter later recalled in one *Fast Company* interview:

> 'I'll never forget,' Lasseter says, 'Steve Jobs was kind of waxing poetically about things and he said, "You know, at Apple when we make a computer, what's the lifespan of it? Maybe three years. In five years it's a doorstop. Technology moves so fast. If you do your job right with *Toy Story*, this thing could last forever."'

> (5.1)

Disney liked *Tin Toy*, and tried to poach Lasseter from Pixar to lead its animation division. But Lasseter was loyal to Jobs, and Disney settled for an agreement with Pixar to make a film for Disney. A string of commercial and critical successes followed, including *Toy Story, A Bug's Life, Toy Story 2, Monsters Inc., Finding Nemo,* and *The Incredibles,* which culminated in Disney's $7.4 billion acquisition of Pixar in 2005.

Sometimes, patience is important when re-entrepreneuring. Jobs waited years for Lasseter's vision to mature. Being on the cutting edge of technology, however, he arguably had time to wait. Sometimes, though, leaders must act much more quickly if they want to seize an opportunity, particularly if the opening emerges outside the company's original value chain.

Mannesmann: An inspired step in the dark

In the late 1980s, Germany's quiet telecoms market was suddenly upended, as the government deregulated fixed-line services and technology pushed the costs of mobile telephony down. (5.2)

With the arrival of cellular technology and a newly unregulated telecoms market, an old German industrial conglomerate, Mannesmann, unexpectedly joined the mobile telephony gold rush, becoming one of the first continental European private sector companies to compete in a sector long-dominated by state-owned telecom incumbents, in this case, with DeTeMobile (Deutsche Telekom).

It was a bold and somewhat surprising move. Founded in 1890, Mannesmann had started life as a steel tube business and then gradually expanded to other sectors, most of which were somewhat related to steel (5.3): iron ore, coal and then, later, mechanical and electrical engineering, plant construction and automotive supply. As a result, analysts did not see Mannesmann's entry into the mobile telephony market coming. After acquiring its mobile communications licence in 1989, Mannesmann formed a subsidiary, Mannesmann Mobilfunk, the following year. With this step, the company was the first private company to enter Germany's telecommunications industry. The firm's boldness paid off: by 1994, Mannesmann Mobilfunk gained a market share of over 40 per cent, even surpassing the former market leader, the recently privatized Deutsche Telekom.

Other companies rushed in after these pioneers. Some were start-ups, such as E Plus. Other new entrants were old-line firms, RWE and Deutsche Bahn, that sensed an opportunity. But many of the old-line companies underestimated the scale of the investment that would be required. By the mid-1990s they had begun to question the wisdom of their telephony adventures, and wanted out.

Ultimately, Mannesmann and Deutsche Telecom's mobile market share exceeded 80 per cent, but Mannesmann's ambitions were not satisfied. Management set their sights on becoming a full-range telecoms supplier with integrated services that included mobile and fixed-line telephony, Internet and e-commerce. But to reach that goal, they would need to launch another new company.

In 1996, the firm formed Mannesmann Arcor, the group's fixed-line telephony and Internet business, as a joint venture between Mannesmann, Deutsche Bank and DB's telecom subsidiary, DBKom. (Deutsche Bank and Deutsche Bahn retained interests in Arcor until 2008 when they sold their residual 8 per cent and 18 per cent respectively to Vodafone.) (5.4)

One contemporary observer attributed Mannesmann's success in its telecoms business to two factors: first, the management had the courage to contemplate a total metamorphosis. They were willing to dispose of mature assets to invest more deeply in this new capital-intensive business. Second, in Mannesmann Mobilfunk, the management had succeeded in creating a new culture suited to the telecom business. (5.5) The group's leaders had realized they did not know much about this new business and were not too proud to seek advice and hire people with relevant experience. To make sure they hired the right people, they gave the leaders of Arcor, their fixed-line acquisition, a free hand to develop and implement their own business concepts, and to hire people from outside the group.

Mannesmann's persistence was handsomely rewarded. When the fixed-line Arcor subsidiary acquired o.tel.o communications in 1999, Mannesmann had achieved its goal of being firmly established as one of the top two telecommunication providers in Germany. (5.6) In less than 10 years, it had become one of Europe's largest private telecom providers. The telecom business had become so successful that a plan was hatched to spin off Mannesmann's older businesses, which still accounted for three-quarters of group revenues, through a stock market flotation under the name of Atecs Mannesmann. (5.7), (5.8)

Before the plans came to fruition, however, Vodafone, an even more aggressive mobile operator that had grown up in the UK, launched a hostile takeover bid for Mannesmann. After a bid battle lasting several months, Mannesmann's supervisory board accepted an improved offer on 4 February 2000 that valued the German company at almost 60 per cent more than its pre-bid market value.

In the case of Pixar and Mannesmann, technology helped open up glamorous new frontiers. Often, however, the re-entrepreneuring opportunity can be much more subtle. Consider, for example, the case of Sir Martin Sorrell at WPP, who rolled up dozens of advertising agencies and public relations firms and forged them into the world's largest publicity and advertising company – and all without ever having written a single idea about how to write an ad or create a publicity campaign.

Migration to value

In 1985, Sir Martin Sorrell, who had recently resigned as the finance director of the advertising and business services group Saatchi & Saatchi took control of WPP (originally known as Wire & Plastic Products), a British wire shopping basket manufacturer.

But Sorrell and his partner Preston Rabl had no intention of sticking to the basket business. As CFO at Saatchi & Saatchi, Sir Martin had been instrumental in realizing the Saatchi brothers' vision of assembling via acquisitions a global business services group embracing everything from advertising to management consulting. When he moved to WPP full-time as CEO in 1986, he intended to do it all over again, by acquiring a succession of small design and sales promotion companies in the UK and the US. As he later recounted in the *Harvard Business Review*:

> We focused on firms specializing in what are called 'below the line' marketing functions. In advertising, 'above the line' is the sexy,

creative, Don Draper stuff. Below the line is the unfancy, unsexy stuff – packaging, design, promotions. Below-the-line agencies never get much attention, but they can be good businesses. We bought 15 of them in the UK and three in the United States, using mostly our shares as financing, and became the largest player on either side of the Atlantic. The stock market liked our strategy, and our market cap kept growing.

In June 1987 the breath-taking scale of Sir Martin's ambitions became apparent when he launched a hostile $566 million takeover bid for J. Walter Thompson (JWT), one of Madison Avenue's most storied advertising agencies.

But Sorrell was not just playing the Saatchis' game all over again. He envisioned WPP as a holding company without the Saatchis' ego. It would keep a low profile in the world of advertising. The business-winning brand names would be those of the star agencies in its portfolio, such as JWT and, subsequently, Ogilvy & Mather (acquired in 1989) and Young & Rubicam (acquired in 2000). (5.9)

Sir Martin saw WPP's job as purely administrative: WPP would relieve the agency leaders of the distractions of financial management, and impose on them some cost discipline, increasing margins from a little below average to a little above. Instead of looking at advertising as a special, creative business where the assets all leave in the elevator every night, his background enabled him to look at JWT and WPP's other acquisitions as businesses that were being operated in a financially sloppy way. A little stronger financial focus was all he needed to cover costs and debt interest and create value for WPP's shareholders.

This is the beauty of re-entrepreneuring: it frees organizations from any mental barriers that might exist. It allows them to think freely and consider opportunities they wouldn't have dared to touch had they been caught within the confines of their current conception of their business. Who would have imagined – except maybe Sir Martin – that in just 30 years, WPP would have morphed from a small, provincial wire basket manufacturer to a global advertising and publicity leviathan with more than 200,000 employees and 3,000 offices operating in 112 countries? In 2018, the company hit a speed bump with allegations of financial impropriety against Sir Martin, after which he stepped down. But that doesn't dilute the fact that he created a formidable advertising giant out of virtually nothing.

Open-minded organizations

As organizations grow and develop, they acquire lives of their own. Their cultures develop their own sub-conscious defence mechanisms, such as habits of mind, prejudices, assumptions, conventions and traditions. Taken together, these defence mechanisms burden organizations with high-degrees of 'path dependence'. In other words, they find it hard to contemplate a future along other lines than its present direction of travel.

All the organizations in this chapter overcame this subconscious 'path dependence' through the adaptive power of a re-entrepreneuring outlook. Abandoning a business model that has served a company well for decades can be a risky strategy. On the other hand, clinging to a traditional business model can sometimes be even riskier. Sensing when the risks of change are lower than the risks of sticking to a tried and true model is the mark of an executive team with good re-entrepreneuring instincts. In the end, it is imagination that is always in the shortest supply, not opportunity or capital.

SUMMARY

- Not all opportunities lie within the organization's core.

- Core competences should be periodically re-evaluated.

- In fast-changing environments, where value chains become both global and fragmented, a company's ability to reconceive its business in a way that moves it to a more profitable position on the value chain can lead to a substantive new competitive advantage.

- Lack of imagination is the entrepreneurs' chief constraint.

6

Re-model

Review your business model before you have to

From a certain angle, a crisis is a gift. A 'burning platform' cuts short debates about whether a change is needed and focuses the organization's resolve about what it must do next. Change can be much more difficult to make if on the surface nothing seems amiss.

Re-entrepreneuring can help an organization free itself from the false sense of security sustained by strict adherence to conventions and routines. It is the right step to take when you realize that what you thought was confidence has deteriorated into a dangerous complacency.

In this chapter, we focus on organizations that were fundamentally happy with their offering and client base but the leadership had a sense that their business models were not well-suited for the competition ahead.

Just as offerings can fall out of sync with the market over time, so too can business models – and once that 'fit' is lost, it can be equally hard to adjust. Successful models tend to become embedded in the culture and the routine of day-to-day operations. Sometimes they acquire the status of fundamental truths about how the market or market segment must be addressed.

For example, retailers once assumed that stores were integral to the retail businesses, and mail order would never account for more than a small fraction of the market. Then along came Amazon and proved the conventional wisdom wrong. Twenty years later, that new idea is now old: even as analysts are consigning physical stores to the graveyard, Amazon is testing physical bookstores, and recently bought Whole Foods, the upscale American grocer.

Organizations like Amazon know they need to keep their business models constantly under review if they are not to be ambushed by model-challenging events, such as a technological breakthrough or an unorthodox competitive move by a close rival or a new entrant. This state of more or less constant vigilance is not an easy existence but it has one plus side: once mastered, it can extend the life of a company decades longer than its peers.

Michelin comes around

If there is a company whose identity is closely linked to its product, it is the French group Michelin, which since 1889 has manufactured tyres for all types of vehicles. Even now the Michelin Man, Bibendum, is the worldwide symbol of excellence for this product.

Confronted for many years by increasingly fierce competitors, especially from Asia, Michelin has placed product innovation at the heart of its strategy. Since the early 2000s, the group's engineers have focused on new industrial processes that have enabled them to innovate not only in tyres, but also in additive manufacturing.

Innovative tyre manufacturing required increasingly complex moulds, but Michelin's teams felt they had reached the limits of what was possible with conventional subtractive techniques. Metal additive manufacturing allows the manufacture of complex mould parts, and in the particular case of Michelin, of metal sipes that form, during moulding, the tread pattern of the tyre, previously unachievable with traditional means.

In 2009, Michelin developed its own machine and industrialized solution because the solutions available on the market were not adapted to the needs of the automotive sector. A few years later, several new innovative tyre lines were launched as the 'MICHELIN Premier' range in the US and 'MICHELIN CrossClimate' in Europe.

The group soon understood that additive metallic manufacturing was a technology with great promise. Many engineers beyond the company said that additive manufacturing represents a major revolution in the history of industrial processes. On the one hand, it allows complex parts to be processed with excellent accuracy and material health. On the other hand, it allows customized mass production on demand.

Not only did additive manufacturing help Michelin innovate the company's traditional core business, business strategists believe it could also eventually open growth drivers in sectors far beyond automobiles: the medical sector, aeronautics, energy and more.

Additive manufacturing appeared so revolutionary that Michelin looked for a way to assert its technological leadership. The group then sought a partner with whom to associate, and they found it in

Fives, a French industrial engineering group with expertise in the design and installation of industrial machinery and equipment.

AddUp, their joint venture, was launched in April 2016 to develop industrial machines and production halls based on the metallic additive manufacturing technology and market them worldwide. The venture's initial goal was to capture 10 per cent of the global market for additive manufacturing equipment within five years (it now represents 800 to 900 machines per year). Along with machines, AddUp aims to offer services and solutions that range from parts (re) design and prototyping to consulting or training.

At a time when mobility is radically changing, when it is not certain that road transportation represents the future of transportation, this Michelin group venture offers a successful example of re-entrepreneuring.

By strengthening its technological leadership, Michelin is preparing its future, not only by offering innovative products and services that enable it to remain a market leader in tyres, but also by seeking new growth opportunities based on its expertise in high-technology materials.

Re-entrepreneuring requires a broader, more outward-looking perspective than conventional management. It depends on attentive listening to weak signals that could herald major changes and phase transitions – and a careful sense of discernment.

The cases of the Japanese automaker Toyota, and of one of its most important parts suppliers, Denso, for example illustrate the opportunity that can be captured when managers are able to think big and wide and reimagine their role in the market.

Toyota: Improving the human/organization interface

Nearly 350,000 people work for Toyota worldwide, each in one of roughly 560 different entities. Given its size and complexity, the firm is not the kind of organization with which one would normally associate such adjectives as nimble, fast or flexible. But Toyota has a history of pioneering developments in organizational design. The Toyota Production System, for instance, turned the automotive – and eventually, the manufacturing – world upside down. The integrated socio-technical system that combined a decentralized management philosophy with a set of lean management practices was enormously influential both within and beyond the automotive industry.

For such a large organization, Toyota is seldom complacent about its position in the global market and strives to stay adapted to a constantly changing environment. These days, however, Toyota managers will tell you that they are looking not just for opportunities to innovate, but to 'be reborn' altogether. Conscious of the limitations of Toyota's existing business models and production processes, and facing such major changes in its market as driverless vehicles, electrification and the Internet of Things (IoT) on the car, executives see a need for change that goes far beyond simple restructuring or realignment.

Today, Toyota managers are focusing on four different projects:

First, they hope to create a culture in which a future for personal mobility without cars is at least conceivable.

Second, they are trying to take a more nimble approach that considers the needs of customers before production efficiency.

Third, they hope to find ways to better integrate smaller organizations within the Toyota group to accelerate their decision-making and execution speeds.

Fourth, they are trying to think beyond individual car models to create a new kind of 'mobility platform' that will be more accepting of innovation and new uses of their vehicles.

To achieve those goals, Toyota has pursued a number of initiatives over the past three years.

- The Open Road Project, started in 2014, considers new options for mobility through conversations with various people outside the automobile industry. The futuristic i-Road, a three-wheeled, two-seater electric vehicle, is one of the first concepts to come out of this project. It is currently being tested in various cities.

- In December 2016, the company launched Toyota Next, a research project focused on co-creating 'human-centred' mobility services with outside partners. Researchers hope Toyota Next will be able to apply innovative technologies and fresh ideas to thinking about personal transportation.

- In January 2016, Toyota launched a Silicon Valley research institute, which will gather together experts in various fields of machine learning and cloud computing. The Toyota Research Institute, as it is called, will use artificial intelligence to improve 'the quality of human life' in various ways: from 'making automobiles safer, more affordable, and more accessible to everyone, regardless of age or ability, . . . to expanding the benefit of mobility technology beyond automobiles, for example to in-home support of older persons and those with special needs.'

- Toyota's 'Connected Strategy' is focused on communication equipment in cars by 2020, including what a mobility 'app store' might look like.

When your largest customer – who also happens to be your former parent and is also your largest shareholder – starts talking about the future and the possibility of radical changes in its marketplace, you listen. Denso, a key Toyota supplier, faced just this situation with Toyota, and immediately responded with its own re-entrepreneuring programme.

Denso: Improving the 'continuous improvement' philosophy

Denso is the world's third-largest auto parts maker, behind Robert Bosch and Continental. Over 151,000 employees work in its 220 units at various locations around the world. It is 25 per cent owned by Toyota but the carmaker now accounts for less than half of its sales.

As they watched Toyota's struggle to develop a new competitive paradigm, Denso's leadership group came to the conclusion that, although in today's fast-changing, unpredictable environment, the 'kaizen' (continuous improvement) management approach Denso shares with Toyota remained necessary, it was no longer sufficient and a more radical process of adaptation was required.

They saw three major environmental challenges – the shrinking of the domestic Japanese market, the company's declining competitiveness in the global marketplace caused by the appreciation of the yen, and a number of threats to industry norms and conventions posed by the Internet of Things.

Denso's solution: the 'Excellent Factory', a radical new approach to manufacturing.

Denso's philosophy takes a zero-based view of the existing manufacturing process. Denso disassembles every sub-routine into its component parts, the compliance of each part with the 'minimum manufacturing required' principle is reviewed, and the parts are reassembled according to a more efficient and flexible manufacturing process.

Following the mantra 'thousands of ideas knocking on the door', employees with different expertise, experience, skills and perspectives were encouraged to gather together, come up with ideas, discuss them and subject them to 'homemade tasting' – the immediate feedback of peers from all over the company. Even when the ideas were imperfect and underdeveloped, they were tested immediately to see if they could work.

In this way, small improvements were made at Denso's factories, and the prototyping process simplified and accelerated: set-up change time was cut by 85 per cent, the installation area reduced by 80 per cent, energy consumption halved, and production costs reduced by a third.

In addition to the Excellent Factory, Denso has developed a Dynamic Products Factory to prepare for the Internet of Things revolution.

The DP-Factory IoT Innovation Lab opened in June 2015 with operations in Japan, North America and Europe. The objectives are to provide useful information to those engaged in manufacturing processes, to liberate employees from routine tasks so they can concentrate their efforts on higher value-added activities, to prevent line stoppages, and to maximize production. The goal here was to boost productivity by 30 per cent between 2015 and 2020, and to apply the lessons learned in the DP-Factory to all Denso factories worldwide.

Re-entrepreneuring ecosystems

No organization is an island. Each sits on at least one, and often several, value chains. Each operates within at least one regulatory and fiscal environment; recruits from several labour markets; competes with local and international rivals; and must adapt to the social, political, economic, financial and technological contexts in which it finds itself.

So to insist that entrepreneurial restructuring must be based on an 'adapted business model' is easier said than done. Adaptation can never be perfect. It is always complex, because there are several links in the chain and they interact with one another in subtle and unexpected ways – there is no way to pre-empt what form those interactions will take and what impact they will have. Also, different parts of the chain acquire more or less weight at different points of time depending on specific situations and circumstances.

The environment to which organizations have to adapt consists mostly of other organizations each of which is also adapting. When a large organization starts re-entrepreneuring successfully, there will be pressure on others in the same group, or on the same value chain, to do likewise. Denso's views of the future have converged with Toyota's, not because the car parts supplier wants to curry favour with its most powerful customer, but because without such a shared view of the future, the integrity of the entire value chain would be in jeopardy.

The tendency for the worldviews of organizations on the same value chain to converge means new business models propagate up and down value chains.

These mutual dependencies on value chains mean organizations co-evolve with environments that include other organizations with which they deal or are otherwise obliged to adapt to. For example, private sector organizations are influenced to some extent these days by the tax regimes to which they are subject. One reason for the US pharma group Pfizer's controversial, subsequently abandoned, 2014 bid for AstraZeneca, of the UK, was thought to be Pfizer's wish to 'invert' to the UK, and become subject to the UK's more favourable tax regime.

Organizations are also shaped by political qualities of their environments and prevailing beliefs about the merits, or otherwise, of government control of or intervention in markets.

Increasingly, organizations are having to take a similar tack to Denso by trying to future-proof themselves from the beginning. The idea is not only to think about how to be efficient now, but how to stay ahead of the technology as it advances. BGI, the Chinese genomic juggernaut, is another organization that is working hard to stay ahead of the curve.

BGI: Taking control of your destiny

The first human genome cost $3 billion to sequence. The job involved 20 universities and research institutes in the US, the UK, Japan, France, Germany, Canada and China, and took 14 years, running from 1990 to 2003.

By 2007, the cost of sequencing a full genome had fallen to $2 million. A decade later it is now under $1,000, and industry insiders say it may soon drop as low as $200. (6.1)

The organization that has done more than any other to bring the price of genome sequencing down is a company known as BGI, which began life as the Beijing Genomics Institute. The organization was founded in Beijing in late 1999 by Wang Jian, Yu Jun, Yang Huanming and Liu Siqi, under the patronage of the Chinese Academy of Sciences (CAS).

In the beginning, BGI had a relatively short-term purpose: to act as China's main participant in the Human Genome Project. As funding dried up following the completion of the Human Genome Project, the founders of BGI had to decide what to do next.

One option, of course, would be to close the operation down. After all, BGI had achieved its objective. However, BGI had built so much valuable intellectual property in the form of equipment and sequencing knowhow, no one at the company felt that would be an attractive option. Instead, they looked for a new role for BGI.

BGI's leaders decided to sell genome sequencing services, but not just for the human genome. Unlike leading genetic research institutes such as the Broad Institute in the US, and Great Britain's Wellcome Trust Sanger Institute, BGI cast its sequencing net much wider. In addition to healthcare, BGI would focus on agriculture and bio-energy.

In time, this has turned into a valuable asset in its own right. Now, thanks to the number and variety of sequencing projects it has undertaken, BGI has amassed the world's largest bioinformatics database. As of 2013, BGI had sequenced more than 57,000 human genomes, more than 6,000 microbe genomes, 5,300 metagenomes, and, in plants and animals, more than 580 species and 28,200 variation genomes (6.2), and in the process has become the world's largest sequencer of human, plant and animal DNA.

It wasn't all smooth sailing, however. In the early days after the completion of the Human Genome Project, the relationship with the bureaucratic and research-orientated CAS was irksome for the young, opportunistic enterprise that valued flexibility, nimbleness and fast reactions. And funds were in short supply: at one stage BGI's headcount fell to 20, compared to 400 at the peak of the Human Genome Project.

But BGI had established a reputation as one of China's major players in biotechnology. In 2002, it earned a place on the cover of *Science*, the weekly journal of the American Association for the Advancement of Science, for sequencing the rice genome. In 2003, it decoded the SARS virus genome and created a kit for detecting the virus. (6.3)

Attracted by an offer of financial assistance from the Hangzhou municipal government, BGI moved to the Zhejiang Province city in east China in 2001.

In partnership with Zhejiang University, BGI founded the James D. Watson Institute of Genome Sciences. The founders intended the institute (named after the co-discoverer with Francis Crick of the double-helix structure of DNA) to become a major centre for research and education in East Asia, modelled on the non-profit Cold Spring Harbor Laboratory on Long Island, New York.

Hangzhou was not the only city that liked the idea of hosting China's emerging bio-engineering champion. In 2007, the city of Shenzhen lured BGI away with a package that included a RMB 90 million grant and the use of a vacant shoe factory building for four years.

The company made the headlines twice in the following year: first, when it published the first human genome of an Asian individual; and second, when it announced that it had ordered 128 DNA sequencing machines from Illumina of San Diego, California. It was a huge order, which made BGI Illumina's single biggest customer in 2010 of the company that dominated the world market for DNA sequencing machines.

The order was a risky move: should advances in sequencing technology continue rapidly – as had been the case for the previous 17 years – BGI faced the possibility that these changes might render these machines obsolete before they had paid for themselves.

BGI's leaders were aware of this danger, but hoped through the Illumina order that they would buy themselves a window of opportunity of at least two years, which would give them the chance to achieve a dominant market position.

Their gamble paid off. The next step – change in sequencing technology – did not come until 2014 with Illumina's announcement of its HiSeq X Ten machine, 40 of which, according to Illumina, could sequence more genomes in one year than had been sequenced by all other sequencers combined, up to that date.

Today, BGI remains on the outside of the genetic technology envelope. It is investing heavily in so-called Next Generation Sequencing, which offers even greater speeds using parallel genomic sequencing, a technology so advanced it is expected to usher in the era of so-called 'personalized medicine'.

Nor was BGI more conservative in its staffing choices. Although BGI researchers keep up with the latest trends in genetic science, the company is not wedded to academic credentials in hiring staff for its commercial operations. It hires young people, even college dropouts, and trains them in its own college, which grants degrees via affiliations with universities. Some staff even live in 'on campus' dorms. In 2013, most earned about RMB 100,000 ($16,500) a year, a good salary in Chinese terms but still far less than their counterparts elsewhere in the world.

BGI's combination of high sequencing volume, low personnel costs and home-grown innovation has done more than carve out a competitive commercial position for the Chinese organization. It is contributing significantly to the advancement of gene-based medicine.

But company strategists have realized that BGI must continue to shift its business model as the technology advances. That is why BGI acquired Complete Genomics (CG) based in Mountain View, CA, for $117.6 million in 2013. Using CG's technology freed BGI from its dependence on Illumina, enabling the company to develop its own range of sequencing machines, beginning with the high-volume next-gen sequencers, BGISEQ–500 and BGISEQ–50 launched in 2015 and 2016 respectively.

Analysts speculate that BGI made this acquisition in anticipation of a shift in value from simply sequencing DNA to selling already sequenced genetic data – 'bioinformatics' – the mountain of genomic data BGI continues to accumulate at a faster rate than any of its rivals. Commenting on the deal, CG's co-founder, Dr Radoje Drmanac, now senior VP of BGI, said:

> There is a great fit. The two companies had the same vision to implement genomics on a massive scale, to sequence millions of human genomes to improve . . . health and prevent diseases. CG has advanced sequencing technology. BGI has the ability to scale it and use it, . . . [given its] access to big markets and funding.
>
> (6.4)

Foreign investors and co-funders include US venture fund Sequoia Capital, and the Bill and Melinda Gates Foundation. Microsoft founder Bill Gates first visited BGI in its old Shenzhen shoe factory headquarters in 2011. He said he was as impressed as much by the informal, collegiate atmosphere of the place, as by the grandeur of BGI's ambitions. Since then, the Foundation has teamed up with BGI on a variety of projects in agriculture and healthcare in Africa.

With offices and outposts all over the world, and a large and growing network of contacts in industry, academia and the not-for-profit sector, BGI is now a global rather than a Chinese organization. Through a combination of its entrepreneurial outlook, its usefully ambiguous public/private status in China, which provides access to state funds with no strings attached, its distinctive high-volume, low-cost business model, and the speed with which it is now adding to an already mountainous genomic database, BGI has carved out for itself a uniquely powerful position in what is likely to prove one of the twenty-first-century's most important industries. The organization seems to have taken to heart the deepest lesson of genetics: adaptability is everything.

SUMMARY

- Re-entrepreneuring is not always about addressing an immediate crisis, but can also mean 'continuous innovation'.

- Re-entrepreneuring can also be a tool for corporate renewal and staying ahead of the curve.

- Committing to re-entrepreneuring means constantly reviewing your business model.

7

Re-organize

Chaotic environments, agile structures

One of the biggest challenges any leader can face is coping with the fast changing environment. In this chapter, we look at how some companies have learned to handle rapidly evolving markets by re-entrepreneuring – reconsidering their core values, revaluating their position in the current environment, and then trying to find an emerging opening in the market the company will be uniquely suited to fill.

In this regard, the question of the company's shape or structure is anything but secondary. Having the right organization is what enables the company to realize its vision, principles and strategy.

Maintaining a re-entrepreneuring perspective can serve as a kind of gyroscopic function for the firm, keeping the company grounded even as its external environment grows more chaotic. By understanding who you are, you can better understand where you need to go. As Jeff Bezos, the CEO of Amazon, puts it, 'The world changes around you and when it changes against you – what used to be a tail wind is now a head wind – you have to lean into that and figure out what to do because complaining isn't a strategy.'

In spite of all those changes in the external environment, Amazon has maintained a strong and consistent culture of entrepreneurship. Bezos has said that three thoughts have guided Amazon since the founding of the e-commerce pioneer in 1993: 'Put the customer first. Invent. And be patient.' Amid so much hectic, sometimes chaotic, change, Amazon has learned to keep its shape. It has sufficient, but not superfluous structure, with greater powers of adaptability than any of its predecessors.

But the Seattle giant is not unique in this respect. In this chapter, we will look at several companies that have learned to use the power of re-entrepreneuring to keep themselves upright when many less-centred companies would have lost their way.[1]

Rules of the game

On 21 January 2013, *World of Tanks*, a massive multiplayer online (MMO) game, set a Guinness World Record for the highest number of players logged onto one MMO server, with 190,541 gamers from all over the world simultaneously locked in combat in this fantasy world.

It was another triumph for Wargaming, the company behind *World of Tanks*. Founded by Victor Kislyi in 1998 in Minsk, Belarus, Wargaming began as a studio for developing turn-based strategy games for PCs, such as *DBA Online* and a sci-fi brand called *Massive Assault*. But it was not enough. After mastering one level of the global business game, Kislyi felt it was time to move to the next challenge, the next big thing in video games: real-time strategy (RTS) games.

In November 2007, Kislyi purchased Arise, a Minsk-based development studio whose programmers and digital artists had extensive experience in RTS games. A year later, Wargaming released its first RTS game, *Operation Bagration*, followed by *Order of War*. But it was not until 2010 that the company had a hit, *World of Tanks*, the company's first multi-modal online game. *World of Tanks* was an instant success in Russia, where it tapped a rich seam of fascination with history, particularly World War 2. User numbers skyrocketed.

Emboldened by the success of *World of Tanks*, Kislyi began to expand the game's geographical reach and position the company as a global player.

It had become clear by 2011 that the company could not prosper under Belarus's strict regulatory environment, so the founder relocated Wargaming's headquarters to Nicosia, Cyprus, a popular destination for Slavic companies looking for a business-friendly jurisdiction. Later that year, he set up offices in Paris, Berlin and San Francisco. In 2012, the firm expanded to Seoul, South Korea, a key market for multiplayer games.

Now Wargaming was in the right place, but it was not yet in the right shape. Changes in fashion occur too quickly in the gaming business for game developers to be entrepreneurial only some of the time. As with many entertainment businesses, success as a gaming company depends on a steady stream of hits. The two games that followed *World of Tanks* had not been as successful as the original, and Kislyi needed a new winner before interest in *World of Tanks* tapered off.

Paradoxically, Kislyi saw he needed a more rigid structure to preserve his company's entrepreneurial spirit as it grew. To make Wargaming more entrepreneurial, he reorganized the company, centralizing the relevant management functions (HR, financial control, accounting, etc.) but leaving the creative aspects decentralized. This move, in which processes and workflows were defined and reporting objectives and responsibilities were spelled out for the first time, liberated Kislyi from day-to-day management, and allowed him to focus on the entrepreneurial challenges.

Turning Wargaming into an efficient, well-ordered yet decentralized organization left the company's creatively independent local studios free to develop exciting new games without worrying about administrative functions.

Since the reorganization, Wargaming has continued to expand and evolve. In November, 2016, Wargaming, SEGA and Creative Assembly formed a strategic partnership, Wargaming Alliance, to launch *Total War: ARENA worldwide*, as its first title. The idea was to provide third-party publishers and developers with the tools, resources and the platform to enter the free-to-play, MMO gaming market. All told, Wargaming's subscriber base now tops 100 million.

In Wargaming's case, the success of the product revealed the weaknesses of the operating model, as well as the strengths of the business model. The product came first; the organizing system came later, when the rapid growth associated with the global success of *World of Tanks* had exposed the weaknesses of the default system of organization.

As companies mature and the organizing systems fall into place, they often end up crippling the entrepreneurial streak that gave them their *raison d'être*. In that sense, the Wargaming case is an aberration rather than the norm.

The unique re-entrepreneurial approach the company took to transition to its next phase of evolution helped it preserve and nurture the qualities from its start-up stage that are important in a creative business like gaming. At the same time, it was able to create a more mature and stable organization with well-functioning processes and functions, somewhat uncharacteristic of a start-up.

So the company can avail of the benefits of scale that come with being a large company without sacrificing the agility and flexibility of a start-up.

Finding the right structure was therefore a question of balance. Unleashing the creativity of the teams on the one hand, making them as autonomous as possible, while keeping a strong infrastructure on which these same teams can rely to have maximum efficiency and impact. The entrepreneurial energy is increased tenfold since the structure of the company supports it, without stifling it. It is a hard balance to achieve, though.

Balance between team autonomy and centralized infrastructure, but also between what constitutes the core value of the organization (and must remain in place, or risk causing the loss of the business) and the elements that can and must change as strategic repositioning takes place.

In any successful adaptation, the key is changing what needs to change and maintaining those factors that retain their value. In the next case, a Chinese mobile phone company saw that although it needed to change its brand and its offer, it saw no need to cut off its original distribution network which was very much against the trend prevalent in the Chinese market at that time. By grafting a new offer and brand to its old distribution network, the company went from an also-ran in China to a market leader all over Asia.

Vivo: How a dark horse got ahead

In telecom, even the strongest incumbents tend not to stay on top for long. Seemingly invincible giants such as Nokia and Motorola were quickly routed when the realities of the market changed. Yet Vivo, a Chinese newcomer that didn't have the brand equity of a Blackberry or a Nokia, has survived and thrived. In just two decades, first as Bu Bu Gao (BBG) and then as Vivo, the company saw the telecom market change beyond recognition. Yet despite having relatively less experience as a handset manufacturer than others and less financial backing, Vivo managed to keep pace with the complex changes happening in the world around it.

Bu Bu Gao, which in Chinese means 'step by step, rise higher and higher', began as an educational electronics manufacturer in 1995. It expanded soon to DVD players, and then to the fixed-line and cordless telephone handset market. In all three segments, competition was fierce but BBG became the market leader by 2000, defeating all major domestic and international companies in China.

In 2004, BBG's former telephone handset business unit, BBG Telecom, led by CEO Shen Wei and his team, launched the 'music mobile' phone. By then, the Chinese mobile phone market was already crowded with major international and local brands. BBG's 'music mobile' targeted youngsters by featuring music functionality, elegant design and mid- to high-end pricing in what was primarily a feature phone market. It stressed 'perception over affordability' and refused to engage in price wars. Thanks to its prowess in manufacturing, the product quality of the phones went down well with Chinese consumers. All these factors coupled with a successful branding strategy, catapulted BBG to the Top 3 in 'the mid-end and above' segment in the Chinese market by 2008.

Just then, the advent of 3G and smartphones disrupted the mobile phone market in China and around the world. By 2011, Apple, Samsung, HTC and Xiaomi had gained an early-mover advantage and looked set to dominate the market in the following decade.

Unlike the top brass at Nokia, Motorola or Blackberry, however, BBG executives thought this was no time for business as usual. They needed a smartphone that would attract the market's attention. They carefully weighed the trade-offs and decided that in order to enter the smartphone era with a bang, they needed to launch a new brand without the old almost dowdy brand associations of BBG. In the short run, this would cost the company brand equity, but in the long run, they calculated, it would give them the best chance to stay a contender in the market.

Along with a new name, Vivo created a distinctive product that focused on young people, which had been a neglected demographic in China. Vivo realized that there was a group of young and trendy smartphone consumers who were not satisfied with entry-level smartphones with basic functions but were not ready to pay a premium price for a top-of-the-line iPhone or Samsung Galaxy.

But Vivo's play for this market was not just a pricing strategy: Vivo developers did not neglect design. In November 2012, Vivo launched Vivo X1, which at a thickness of 6.55 mm was the slimmest phone at that time. It was also the world's first smartphone embedded with a Hi-Fi music processor chip.

In the short run, BBG, now Vivo, paid a high price for rebranding. In 2010 and 2011, carriers in China heavily subsidized smartphones to nudge buyers. This left these partners stuck with a huge inventory of the unpopular older generation feature phones under the BBG brand name. But Vivo stuck by its loyal distribution partners to unload the stock completely and bear the costs.

This turned out to be a crucial decision for Vivo. At the time, actual physical stores were out of fashion. Hadn't the success of other smartphone makers, such as Xiaomi, shown that a direct sales model was the best way to sell smartphones? In fact, having access to stores through its distribution partners, and giving them equal pricing terms as those offered on Vivo's online sales channel, gave Vivo a winning edge that was not easy to replicate.

The new phone was a hit, and not just in China; consumers across Asia also took to the brand. As a result, it sold 30 million phones in 2014, doubling its sales over the previous year. In 2016, the number stood at 70 million.

Today, Vivo has become one of the Top 3 smartphone brands in both China and India, beating the likes of Apple and Xiaomi.

Vivo might look completely different from BBG, but it is important to note that although the company had changed its name and its product, it had stuck to a set of core rules that had served it well from the beginning:

Fight no price wars. While other Chinese brands frequently engage in price wars to enter new markets and gain an edge over rivals, Vivo never competes on price.

Insist on product excellence. Vivo has built a strong supply-chain management and quality assurance team, supplemented by self-owned manufacturing facilities, to ensure that its product achieves high standards and supply remains reliable. Vivo chose to be less dependent on external ODMs (original design manufacturers) and built stronger direct relationships with its key component suppliers. This gives it the competitive edge when high-quality supplies become tight and product quality could be at risk.

Stand by your allies. In its earlier incarnation as BBG and even as Vivo, the company built and reinforced its independent distribution system in the open market to maintain a profitable business model for its distribution partners and to avoid channel conflicts. While other brands also depend on mobile carriers' subsidies for market development, transactional behaviour on both sides limited the strength of the relationship. Vivo's decision to stand by its distributors by buying the discontinued phones has paid off with the development of an extended ecosystem united by common business goals and cultural beliefs.

To this day, Vivo subscribes to the original BBG ethos about maintaining quality and not indulging in price wars of any kind. Nor did the company make Faustian bargains with carriers as other handset manufacturers did. It nurtured its distribution system to the extent that the independent distributors were steeped in the Vivo culture. On the other hand, its strong relationships with distributors helped Vivo remain flexible as market needs changed. These relationships have proved to be vital in Vivo's growth story.

Vivo literally reinvented this industry, when it was not especially intended to *a priori*. What led to its success is, again, a question of right balance. Balance between core values that are part of the corporate identity which leaders have never negotiated on the one hand, and the search for the best fit to the context and the market on the other hand.

Of course, part of re-entrepreneuring is not just taking advantage of your own capabilities but taking advantage of the capabilities of others in your ecosystem, as the saga of Didi, a Chinese ride-sharing app, shows. Whether it was cash, technology or market access, Didi always somehow found precisely what it needed, when it needed it.

Didi Chuxing's ride to the top

When Cheng Wei and several Alibaba 'classmates' (as colleagues are known at China's e-commerce giant) left in 2012 to set up a ride-hailing venture they named Didi Dache ('honk honk taxi') they were one of about 30 Chinese start-ups with the same idea.

Cheng's inspiration was Hailo – a UK company that worked with London's licensed black cabs. Cheng thought the Hailo model would work in China, with its 2 million yellow-stripe taxis. His first target was Shenzhen, the industrial heartland of southern China, which had a reputation for a light-touch regulatory regime. But in this case, trust in Shenzhen's liberal credentials was misplaced; Didi's ride-hailing app was banned by the municipal authorities as soon as it was launched.

Undeterred, Cheng looked elsewhere for a foothold in the now-crowded marketplace. When Yaoyao Taxi, a rival app backed by a US venture fund, obtained an exclusive licence to recruit drivers at

Beijing's international airport, Cheng decided to counter the strategy with an aggressive recruitment drive at Beijing's largest rail station.

He also widened Didi's offering, by adding to its ride-hailing service such features as private cars, limousines, car pooling and ordering a chauffeur when you have over-indulged, and don't want to drive home. It caught on quickly with users, but not with drivers.

Didi wasn't as well capitalized as some of its rivals and couldn't afford to adopt the common recruitment practice of giving smartphones with its app to cab drivers. This resource constraint obliged Didi to target younger drivers who already had smartphones – a problem in the short run that turned out to be an advantage: because of their greater familiarity with social media, these drivers were more likely to spread the word about Didi.

Another stroke of luck was a blizzard in Beijing in late 2012. The extreme weather made it impossible to hail a cab on the street, so people used the app and Didi got them home. Didi's orders exceeded 1,000 in a day for the first time. A Beijing venture capital firm took notice and bought a 20 per cent stake in the business for $2 million. (7.1)

Cheng acknowledges the role luck has played in Didi's initial success. 'If it didn't snow that year, maybe Didi wouldn't be here today,' he suggested in an interview with *Bloomberg Businessweek* in October 2016. (7.2)

Whether through luck or design – or as in Didi's case, a little bit of both – by 2016, the initial crowd of ride-app challengers had thinned to a handful, among which was Kuaidi Dache ('Fast Taxi'). Kuaidi acquired a major competitive edge over Didi when it won backing from Didi's *alma mater*, Alibaba, one of China's 'big three' web-based groups. Knowing that backing from a 'big three' company could be decisive, Cheng sought and won the support of Tencent, the social networking and media content group.

Cheng appealed to Tencent's founder, Pony Ma, for help and Ma came through, lending him 50 engineers and a thousand servers.

But Didi was still losing money and needed more capital, so Cheng flew to the US in November 2013 to seek new investors. He had no luck. 'We'd burned a lot of money,' he recalled to *Bloomberg Businessweek*. 'Investors were like, "Whoa".'

Didi solved its under-capitalization problem accidentally, as a consequence of the unexpected success of a promotion by Tencent in early 2014. The 'Red Packet' promotion, named after the colour of the envelope in which small cash sums are traditionally sent to friends and family over the Lunar New Year holidays, enabled users of Tencent's WeChat Wallet to send their gifts with smartphones.

This alerted Tencent to the enormous potential of payments by smartphone. It saw Didi, which was already allowing passengers to pay drivers with WeChat's cashless service, as a prime application of WeChat's cash-system, and invested more money in the company.

Alibaba followed suit. It invested more in Kuaidi, and linked it into its mobile payment system, AliPay. In a pitched battle for market dominance, the rivals spent huge sums on discounts and subsidies in early 2014.

But before they could settle that contest, Uber launched its Chinese app, and competition heated up even further.

The US invader was a formidable opponent. It experimented with a variety of tactics to differentiate its app. Its operations in different cities were run independently, so that managers could adapt the offer to local conditions, it introduced service/product variants, such as

People's Uber, an option to pick up passengers just for a share of the gas money, and it deployed innovative marketing campaigns such as Uber boats, and Uber rickshaws. By the beginning of 2015 it had a third of China's private car-hailing market.

Eventually, however, Didi beat Uber, thanks to its intimate knowledge of the Chinese consumer. Uber walked into China with its global app, which did not allow for small adjustments like using your phone to order a cab for your grandma who might not be a smartphone user. Didi's did, along with a slew of other features designed with the Chinese consumer in mind. Second, in China, drivers often use multiple ride-sharing apps to maximize their chances of finding a fare. Didi upped the ante by wooing drivers away from Uber by offering them incentives. It was a tactic taken very seriously by Didi's senior management: every morning, Cheng reviewed which subsidies and discounts had worked the previous day, and then fine-tuned the offers. When Didi offered them the better deal, drivers had no reason to stick to Uber.

With Uber's then-CEO Travis Kalanick casting covetous looks at the Chinese market, the blood-letting between the local companies began to seem self-defeating. In February 2015, Didi and Kuaidi merged. Didi had the market share edge by then, and its shareholders ended up with 60 per cent of the enlarged company, with Cheng still CEO.

In May 2015, the new Didi tried to break the deadlock with Uber by offering to give away 1 billion yuan in rides. Uber followed suit. To further up the ante, Didi contemplated an outflanking attack on Uber's home market in the US by investing $100 million in an Uber rival, San Francisco-based Lyft, and bought shares in Ola in Bangalore,

India, and Grab (formerly GrabTaxi), which was based in Singapore but operated throughout South East Asia.

These four companies – Didi (renamed Didi Chuxing 'Honk, Honk Commute' in September 2015), Lyft, Ola and Grab – were billed by some as an 'anti-Uber alliance'.

Back in China, the two antagonists continued to burn cash at an alarming rate. 'It was like an arms race,' Cheng told *Bloomberg Businessweek* reporters. 'Uber was fundraising, we were also fundraising'. Didi replenished its coffers by issuing $4 billion worth of shares to Apple, among others in May 2016. Meanwhile, Uber raised $3.5 billion from Saudi Arabia's Public Investment Fund.

It was a re-run of Didi's earlier struggle with Kuaidi and it was clear to both companies that it couldn't last indefinitely. Uber's board, unhappy that they were losing $1 billion in China every year, prodded Kalanick to accept Didi's offer.

In August 2016, Didi acquired Uber China for $1 billion in cash and an 18 per cent stake in Didi; not a conclusive result, but one usually described as a victory for the home team against a formidable foreign invader.

Today, Didi Chuxing is the most valuable private company in the world, but executives may not be satisfied with that ranking: recent reports indicate that the company is preparing for a rematch with their old nemesis, this time in Mexico. In South East Asia too, Didi and SoftBank have invested $2 billion in Grab. (Uber has since given up on South East Asia and merged with Grab.)

'We're the craziest companies of our times,' Cheng said of Didi and Uber after the deal to *Bloomberg Businessweek*. 'But deep in our heart we are logical. We know this revolution is a technology revolution and we are just witnessing the very beginning.'

What gave Didi strength was its ability to remain agile, to the point of surprising everyone with unpredictable tactical moves. In a context of shifting markets and accelerated technological progress, this capacity is a central asset. But leaders have given themselves the means to focus on creativity and surprise, adopting an agile structure. In doing so they ensured the success of the company.

SUMMARY

- As markets change, it is important to decide which organizational structures and cultural values you should keep and which you should adjust.

- Re-entrepreneuring is often a balance between rigidity and entrepreneurial qualities like creativity and agility.

- In some cases it is the balance between the core values and principles and the demands of the market.

- Re-entrepreneuring often means unpredictable moves and challenging the status quo combined with a hard, unflinching focus on creativity.

- Technology and ecosystem partners make changes easier to implement, which means that structural decisions need to be made more quickly than ever.

8

Re-envision

Imagining and creating limitless possibilities

The objective of any organization is to create new value that would not have been created without it. How value is perceived and measured will vary from sector to sector, but the principle that any organization is only as good as the value it creates applies just as much to non-commercial and non-governmental organizations (NGOs) as it does to business. (8.1)

This is why a re-entrepreneurial mind-set can help any organization break free of any of those invisible constraints that bind it and hold it back it from achieving its true potential.

One case in point is the Dutch Kidney Foundation, which had acted as a conventional health charity for over 50 years before setting itself free through re-entrepreneuring. Thanks to its courageous re-entrepreneuring work, DKF was able to completely re-envision its role in improving the lives of people suffering from kidney disease. Under the leadership of a visionary director, DKF went beyond just raising funds for research to become an investor in its own right. The DKF story below shows that once an organization takes its blinkers off, it can achieve all kinds of goals previously deemed impossible.

Neokidney: The re-entrepreneuring of a charity

Until 2010, the Dutch Kidney Foundation (DKF) operated like a typical health charity. It raised funds to support research, kept kidney disease patients informed about treatments and scientific progress, lobbied the government, and raised social awareness about kidney disease. DKF raised money to fund scientific research, educate patients, lobby the government on occasion and generally raise societal awareness.

Yet despite decades of conscientious effort, DKF was making no headway. The technology had not changed in decades and the problems of kidney disease were getting worse. By 2010, the number of people with kidney disease had topped 2 million worldwide and the numbers were growing 5 per cent each year. Even in an advanced country like the Netherlands, one in six people who have kidney disease and are on dialysis won't make it through the year. Other existing treatments were also of limited value. Kidney transplants can restore 80–90 per cent of kidney function, but they last only 10–15 years, require a lot of medication, and patients must wait a minimum of 3–4 years for a donor. Hemodialysis, another alternate treatment, requires the patient to take a variety of medications, many with unpleasant side effects. And for patients on conventional dialysis, the prognosis is not much better than when the first dialysis machines were developed in the 1940s.

Then in the late 2000s, DKF found a model for a new approach. The foundation got involved with BioMedical Materials (BMM), a government-backed public–private partnership that brought together universities, companies and charities to realize long-term goals in the fields of tissue engineering and stem cell technology. DKF's work with BMM led it to set two important new goals for itself.

The first goal was to support kidney-related stem cell research. Reports of success at MIT in the US in growing live tissue from stem cells had increased optimism about the feasibility of growing an artificial but still biological kidney.

However, DKF recognized that this breakthrough might take some time to arrive. And dialysis, as DKF director Tom Oostrom often points out, may save your life, but is no life. In the meantime, they would pursue a second goal: to produce a mechanical, wearable dialysis machine. A desperate shortage of donated kidneys meant that for the foreseeable future, a great many patients would continue to depend on dialysis. Oostrom wanted to make dialysis bearable by making dialysis machines wearable. This would give patients more freedom and allow them to adapt their therapy to their lives rather than their lives to their therapy, as they must now do.

The positive news out of MIT, frustration at the lack of organ donors and lack of progress in improving dialysis, and BMM's emergence in the Netherlands as a focal point for tissue engineering, led DKF to the novel idea of launching a for-profit business to create an artificial kidney. This was a turning point for DKF in two senses: first, in setting a clear target, and second, in pursuing the target actively, by forming a company, rather than passively, by providing financial support for scientific research, the typical practice of a medical science foundation.

DKF leaders knew it might take researchers 20–30 years to learn how to grow kidneys from stem cells. In the meantime, they thought, steps could be taken to liberate kidney patients from their dependence on clinic-based dialysis with a wearable artificial dialysis machine. The idea of a wearable device went back to the 1970s, but progress had been slow, perhaps because a device that could be used anywhere did not represent an attractive market for existing suppliers of dialysis services. The maths was simple and too compelling for the suppliers to ignore: dialysis devices accounted for less than €10 billion of the €60 billion dialysis market. Earnings from dialysis clinics made up the rest, which meant the market leaders had no incentive to develop a device for home use.

DKF strategists began to believe that this market failure obliged the foundation to invest directly in a project to develop a 'wearable' device. Oostrom didn't see this as entrepreneurial, but as re-entrepreneurial – a return to DKF's founding mission: to alleviate the pain of living with kidney failure.

However, DKF's subsequent discussions with patients revealed that in any case, patients would prefer a portable to a wearable device, because a wearable device would constantly remind them of their illness. It would also be more difficult to develop, because there were many technical problems that had to be resolved before they could perfect the wearable device, including permanent vascular access and miniaturization, which had yet to be figured out. However, the development of a portable dialysis machine was already technologically feasible. 'We knew that there was new technology to make the dialysis machine . . . much smaller, like the size of a shoebox,' Oostrom recalled. Yet, because of a market failure, this device had not been built.

A portable device would still be life-changing, DKF executives realized. 'It means you can take the machine with you. You can dialyse at home. You can take it on holidays. You can take it wherever you want,' Oostrom said. 'At the moment, because of the size of that machine, you have to go three times a week to the hospital,' he said. 'At the moment, the patient has to adapt his life to the treatment, to go to the dialysis centre. We would like the treatment to adapt to the life of the patient, so the patient has his life, his freedom back.'

Instead of donating money to academic researchers, DKF started a new foundation, the New Kidney Foundation, and that group formed a company, Neokidney.

'When we started this company . . . we got a lot of questions, and one of the main comments was, 'That's risky that you started the company.' And my answer always is, 'What's risky is to fund fundamental research, but still you have to do it,' Oostrom recalled. In fact, he said, in his opinion, it was in some respects less risky – but it was new. 'It was new for the world for charities, for the world of foundations.'

Neokidney looked for the crucial elements of an artificial kidney, such as absorbents, membrane filters and miniaturization, and reached out beyond the domain of kidney research to other industries that dealt with similar technical challenges: they turned to the water purification industry, for example, for the state of the art in membrane filtration, and to high tech sectors for miniaturization processes. DKF called this process 'search and development', as opposed to research and development.

DKF's pragmatic re-entrepreneuring approach echoed an earlier Dutch pioneering effort in World War 2, when Willem Kolff, a medical internist in Leiden, developed the first artificial kidney, in an effort to extend the life of a young man who was dying of renal failure. He too first identified what he needed, looked around for parts that could fit the bill, and cobbled together his artificial kidney prototype out of parts of a German bomber, cellophane from a local butcher, and a water pump from a Model T Ford.

When completed, the portable dialysis machine should have economic benefits (a year on the portable device should cost at least 43 per cent less than conventional clinic dialysis, bringing the total cost down from €92,000 to €52,600, according to Neokidney's analysis), and provide an enormous improvement in the dialysis patient's quality of life. In conventional dialysis, toxins begin accumulating in the blood as soon as a dialysis session is over. The patient gets progressively sicker until the next session. The more often patients are dialysed, the more they can live normal lives: with a portable dialysis machine a patient can dialyse him- or herself each night.

The introduction of such machines will transform the dialysis market and oblige suppliers of clinic-based services to develop their own machines or lose their role in the market. It remains to be seen how they will adapt and how health systems will absorb what will become largely redundant clinic-based capacity. It seems likely, however, that the arrival of the portable machine will push companies that provide dialysis services to switch their focus from clinics to devices, triggering a surge in the development of better portable devices and adding momentum to the search for the holy grail of the bio-kidney.

The DKF took the lead in raising the first round of financing for its Neokidney project as well as the second round 18 months later. In what may turn out to be among its most significant achievements, it has persuaded health insurers to rethink their roles too, to move beyond being simply payers for dialysis services, to being investors promoting the development of a device that promises to reduce the cost of dialysis permanently.

DKF's pitch to insurers caught them by surprise. Most health insurers have short-term financial goals, centred on annual premium negotiations. They are unused to considering long-term investments, in innovative technologies that may or may not begin to reduce claims several years hence.

Indeed, one could say, as one Neokidney observer put it, that insurance companies are 'allergic to innovation', because in their experience, it is usually associated with higher costs; expensive new treatments, methodologies and devices that improve the quality of life of the insured but increase the cost of claims.

National healthcare systems are under cost pressure the world over as the average ages of populations rise. This has made health insurance companies very conservative, and reluctant to invest in innovation. That things were different in the mental space the DKF created round Neokidney was demonstrated by the fact that no fewer than five competing health insurance companies agreed to invest in Neokidney.

Neokidney is already being approached by major players interested in investing in the project. Such approaches are welcome, but it will be a condition of such involvement that the Neokidney will be taken to market.

The novelty of the DKF approach, which could be emulated by other health charities, is not so much the creation of a company, as the re-conception of its role as a champion of kidney patients. The DKF was innovative in starting with what it wanted to achieve, and thinking carefully about what would be needed to achieve it. It may not require the best science, or the best scientists. It may simply be, as it was in this case, the recombination of existing technologies into novel configurations.

This new conception of the health charity's role has been described by observers as a shift from 'sponsoring research, to investing in moonshots'. Cutting-edge philanthropists now want to define what they want to achieve, work out what is needed to achieve it, and back the firms or researchers most likely to satisfy such needs. They are still very interested in fundamental research, of course, but they are devoting much more attention now to getting promising new treatments to patients more quickly.

Of course, the potential reward is not without a new set of risks. No one could accuse a charity of being irresponsible with donors' money if it backs eminent scientists, and trusts them to do good work, but the research somehow doesn't pay off. But when the charity raises funds to finance its own moonshot, as DKF has done with Neokidney, there's a risk of reputational damage should it fail to reach the moon.

A commercial venture also faces the risk of being beaten to the market by a competitor with a better product. Oostrom knows that is a possibility, but he is not too concerned.

An important difference between the charity and the corporate sectors is that 'value' for charities, and for DKF in this case, is the well-being of the clients. Questions might be asked, in the corporate sector, about a potential conflict of interest, and if DKF had conventional shareholders, it would be in the latters' interests for DKF to favour and promote the Neokidney even if another company came up with a better portable device.

But DKF will be delighted if the Neokidney attracts competing devices. More choice will be of benefit to kidney disease patients and competition will stimulate further advances in the science and technology, Oostrom argues.

Begin with a hypothesis

We have suggested that a distinctive feature of an entrepreneurial outlook is its openness, its inclination to look further and wider for inspiration, opportunity, solutions or knowhow. But you can't simply observe and expect inspiration to emerge unbidden from what you see. Scientific breakthroughs do not begin with observation. They begin with provisional conjectures extrapolated from current knowledge that are subsequently tested. It is the same with 're-entrepreneuring'. Leaders, in such a case, look beyond their current reality toward possible recombinations of their current assets.

Such constraints are often not as restrictive as they are made out to be. In fact, the constraint can help focus and channel, rather than frustrate, the opportunity search.

The first step in re-entrepreneuring in an organization is to see it as an entrepreneur would see it: not as a solid, relatively stable system for creating value, but as a fluid, flexible portfolio of tangible and intangible assets that can be reconfigured and redeployed in all sorts of novel ways that are restricted only by the company's organizational DNA.

A re-entrepreneuring audit can help to establish what the organization might become rather than what it is. It is concerned with potential. When an organization faces adaptive challenges, it tends to be fearful of moving too far from the familiar and proven, and underestimates its strengths. It should take the time to map out all its assets. They are often more numerous and more adaptable than is generally believed.

For example, organizations know a lot more and have access to even more data and information than they might imagine. They need to step back (*reculer*) and see if these dormant and unacknowledged assets enable them to go forward more strongly (*mieux sauter*).

This kind of entrepreneurial asset-mapping begins by identifying assets of various kinds – human and financial capital, IP, data, tangible assets, technical knowhow, reputation, brands, etc. The same audits can be performed on other forms of capital or assets – structural, customer and financial capital, real estate, data, intellectual property, reputation and brand.

A re-entrepreneuring audit can reveal unsuspected strengths and, by undermining the belief that what the organization is doing is the only thing it can do, loosen the constraints on thinking, preparing the ground for re-entrepreneuring. No values are attributed to the audited assets at this stage, because their value, in re-entrepreneuring, will only become apparent later when an opportunity has been identified.

Opportunity hunting

The purpose of a re-entrepreneuring audit isn't to constrain the hunt for opportunity, but to reveal the true extent of the opportunity set, which is usually much larger than it would have seemed before the exercise.

The key question in opportunity hunting is 'given what we are and what we can do, and what we could be and could do, what sort of opportunities are open to us to become something more than we are now?' The answer to this question will depend just as much on the resources the organization could obtain or obtain access to as the resources it already possesses.

SUMMARY

- Re-entrepreneuring begins with self-knowledge.
- Organizations must be objective in their self-assessment via a re-entrepreneuring audit.
- Opportunity hunting is its fundamental mission.

9

Own the future

Don't ask what tomorrow might hold. Imagine it. Make it happen.

The future is not made by scientists and technologists. They supply the building blocks for a set of possible futures. A second, sometimes overlapping, group builds it.

The entrepreneurs who make the actual future include, but are not limited to, the heroic industrialists lionized by Schumpeter: the Vanderbilts, Carnegies and Rockefellers. Entrepreneurs come in less illustrious guise, too. We have argued in this book that it is the amount of entrepreneuring activity going on, not the number of recognizable entrepreneurs in an organization, that will determine whether the organization is more or less creative and adaptable. Entrepreneuring is not the sole domain of a special set of people considered entrepreneurs. Everyone has the potential to be entrepreneuring – even large organizations seldom noted for such qualities can suddenly become more creative and adaptable. Not only by bringing in entrepreneurs from outside the firm, but by reaching back to their own origins, when they were fresh, new, vigorous and on the look-out for opportunities, reawakening those forgotten attributes of youth, adventurousness and adaptability.

We call this rediscovery of youth 're-entrepreneuring'.

Of course, none of this is easy. In this chapter, we will look at the case of Oticon, a Danish hearing aid company that lost its way, rediscovered it through a re-entrepreneuring process, lost it again, and now has rediscovered it once more. Then, to sum up, we will conclude with 5 principles we've learned about re-entrepreneuring.

Projects first, then cultures

This process of rediscovery is not about cultural change, not directly at any rate. It is about doing things differently and doing different things. Culture change is a consequence, not a prerequisite of successful re-entrepreneuring.

If the only entrepreneurial achievements celebrated in an organization belong to the organization's founders, you can bet that there is not much present-tense entrepreneurship going on. In such a 'mature' organization, entrepreneuring is seen as a youthful, reckless way of thinking that the firm has long since outgrown. Strictly speaking, that is correct. You cannot turn the clock back and start again from scratch.

Re-entrepreneuring begins with the recognition that you do not have to start from scratch. You can find new opportunities in the organization's current set of skills, knowledge, networks, and other assets by looking at them from an angle that is less satisfied with today's accomplishments and less sanguine about the virtues of maturity. But note: re-entrepreneuring is very different from injecting entrepreneurs/entrepreneurial spirit into the company. The first proposition works (i.e. re-entrepreneuring) and the second one does not (i.e. injecting entrepreneurs/entrepreneurial spirit into the company). Re-entrepreneuring is about activating the entrepreneurial thinking that is already there, latent, in the company.

Paradoxically, however, the new awareness of the assets the organization already possesses demanded when re-entrepreneuring must often be accompanied by a break from the established organizational structure. One of the best known and most controversial approaches discussed in management literature is the 'spaghetti organization', also known as 'spaghetti management', pioneered by hearing aid manufacturer Oticon and carried on today by another organization founded by Oticon veterans, OM.

Oticon's spaghetti management

In 1904, Hans Deman, a Danish businessman, learned that the Danish-born Queen Alexandra of England wore an American-made hearing aid to her 1902 coronation. Hoping the same device could help his hearing-impaired wife lead a better life, he ordered one for her. (9.1)

Impressed with the device, he started a business importing American hearing aids to Denmark, a business that eventually grew into one of the world's top hearing aid manufacturers.

Over the next eight decades, the Deman family's determination to help the hearing impaired led them to build their firm, now called Oticon, into the world's second-largest supplier of hearing aids, and a technology leader. It introduced the world's first ear-level digital hearing aid to the market in 1996, and in 2016 launched the world's first Internet-connected hearing aid, Oticon opn. The opn, one of the first health appliances powered by the Internet of Things technology, can manage several sound sources at once and scan the environment 100 times per second, to analyse and balance each sound individually.

But in the late 1980s, the company had lost its way. When Lars Kolind was appointed CEO in 1988, Oticon was losing money. Kolind's solution began conventionally: he cut headcount and other costs, and increased productivity. Inside two years, he had returned the firm to profitability.

But he still wasn't satisfied. On New Year's Day, 1990, Kolind issued a memo to staff that took the company in a radical new direction: Oticon needed 'breakthrough' products. To develop them would require a combination of 'audiology, psychology and imagination'. He told staff they had to 'think the unthinkable, and make it happen', and that in the organization of the future 'staff would be liberated to grow personally and professionally and . . . become more creative, action-oriented and efficient'. He had concluded that the enemy of the organization was organization itself, and concluded with the announcement that he had decided to abolish Oticon's formal organization.

In the Kolind managerial vision, the project replaced the function or process as the organizational unit. Project teams would form, disband and reform. Project 'leaders' (anyone who has an idea) compete with each other for resources and people. A Project 'owner' (a member of the top management team who likes the idea) gives advice and support, but makes few decisions.

There were no titles or offices. 'We give people freedom to do what they want,' Kolind told *Fast Company*. (9.2) 'We are developing products twice as fast as anyone else . . . We're not fast on the surface; we're fast underneath.' When one project got so big that it became 'organized', Kolind stepped in and broke it up in a rare top-down management intervention. 'It was total chaos,' Kolind recalled proudly. 'Within three hours, 100 people had moved.' He said one of the main jobs of management is to 'keep the company disorganized'.

Kolind wasn't a conventional leader. He rarely issued commands, apart from urging employees to 'think the unthinkable', and formulated no strategies, unless his declaration that 'we need breakthroughs' can be construed as such. His single rule was that there were no rules. People should simply 'flock' to the projects that seemed the most promising or they found the most interesting. The conventional management wisdom was that managers should try to reduce uncertainty and variation. Kolind argued that the organization could actually stimulate innovation by distributing uncertainty and variety rather than trying to reduce it.

When Kolind resigned as President in May 1998 after a decade in charge, he left the company in excellent health. The hearing aid market was static in the 1990s, but Oticon's sales and profits rose strongly. In October 2000, *Forbes Global* ranked its parent William Demant Holding (WDH) among the world's 20 best small companies.

WDH's stock price had quadrupled over the previous 12 months (the stock price on 1 October 1999 was DKK 21.219 and on

2 October 2000 it stood at DKK 84), and the profits of the company (of which Oticon was the only asset, at the time) had grown by 25 per cent in each of the previous eight years.

Sadly, Kolind's vision did not survive much longer. By the late 1990s, Oticon's success had begun to attract more competition, and distributors' expectations rose. They began to favour suppliers with broader product lines than Oticon offered.

The 'spaghetti organization' also had some less attractive features that made it unstable over time. Some researchers found that coordination and knowledge-sharing suffered. At the same time, selective intervention by the top management also hurt morale and led to some employee frustration. Unhappy staff saw a management style characterized by frequent, erratic interventions that clashed with the company's own espoused culture of empowerment and responsibility. Some saw a need for a counter-revolution within the company that reclaimed the high ground for hierarchy and bureaucracy. Others believed the structure-less structure had outgrown its usefulness for the business.

Niels Jacobsen replaced Kolind as CEO in 1998 and shifted the focus to boosting volume. Oticon Holding acquired the Swiss company, Bernafon, in 1997, as part of a new multi-brand strategy, and changed its name to William Demant Holding.

Under Jacobsen's leadership (1998–2008), Oticon became a full-line supplier, with a single software platform serving different market segments. To support the volume business, marketing and R&D activity was split between three teams, the value-market, the premium market, and the paediatric and severe hearing loss markets. However, the company retained the project-based approached, with sales, marketing and R&D all on each team.

Jacobsen saw the lack of a defined hierarchy as leading to wasteful consensus-based decision-making that had led to numerous meetings, a lack of clear responsibilities, and slow processes. The culture of informal information sharing had had the unintended consequence that people were not used to sharing information without eye contact.

He argued that a more formal structure, supported by a culture change and a more formal knowledge sharing process, was needed, and set up Project Dawn in April 2010. Project Dawn included unveiling a modular product development platform based on 'core assets' that could be combined in different products, akin to a modular automotive platform. The 2010 reorganization was deliberately designed as a break with earlier assumptions and practices and was seen as such by the employees.

Yet until 2010, much of the spaghetti organization still survived. Employees often had several jobs, and were free to decide what they did, and when. They could also choose working hours and training needs. But WDH and Oticon management came to the conclusion that for complex technology projects, combinations of specialized knowledge were often needed.

The demand for specialized knowledge was also being driven by intense technological competition in the hearing aid industry. New features or services were soon copied and customers found it hard to differentiate between products. New products or services were introduced, with ever shorter development times.

When Søren Nielsen was appointed Oticon President in 2008, the board gave him explicit instructions to improve profitability. Margins had been declining, R&D expenses had exploded, and the company was plagued by product launch problems. In particular, Nielsen focused on improving development efficiency, including the company's approach to innovation, through moves that took out more of the old Oticon spaghetti.

One of his first initiatives, Project Dawn, introduced more specialization, giving strict roles and responsibilities for each employee, based on cost-effective innovation. As an Oticon employee explained, 'the good solution is not just the one that performs best. You quickly learn that the good solution is the one that is cheapest, and good enough. That is the art when you're an engineer.'

Now, the company permitted only limited scope for starting projects outside a unit. One employee grumbled, 'Today we sit in different functions and make partial deliveries. That works fine in a sausage factory, but if you want to develop something new, it is very difficult to fit the puzzle pieces together.'

To moderate the potentially stifling effect of the new order, top management introduced the annual 'Inventors Cube' awarded to individuals or teams for patentable inventions, and the three-hour, twice yearly 'Demo Day' at which engineers demonstrate what they are working on to other employees.

To support more effective incremental innovation, managers adapted an Agile 'Scrum' process. But some employees resented the new programme. They felt the use of Scrum prescribed their use of their own time and made it hard to find time to innovate, and to help colleagues on other teams.

We were better at helping each other before. Now that more are using Scrum they're more locked into their own work. When I ask for help, I am told to talk to the project manager, even though the task may only take that person two hours while it would take me four days.

Mutual help had also long been part of the culture. The 'spaghetti organization' encouraged flexibility and risk-taking, and the non-hierarchical organization required personal networks. The 2010 re-organization introduced a 'core business hours' concept. Employees had to be present between 9.00 am and 3.00 pm. Previously, employees did not need to report when they were present, or for how long. This was deemed to be a weakness in a culture of many meetings and face-to-face information sharing.

By 2016, little of the old spaghetti culture had survived. 'It's still OK to ask questions about everything and [to] have opinions about everything. [But] when the organization is divided into silos, it suddenly becomes OK to veto everything. It becomes an "us and them" organization,' said an employee.

But the old Oticon spirit isn't entirely gone: there is a Danish organization that has inherited some of the company's re-entrepreneuring DNA – Oticon Medical (OM), a separate business with linkages to the parent and a sharp focus on cutting-edge technology. OM was formed in 2007 with Jes Olsen, a 20-year Oticon veteran, as CEO.

The idea behind the spin-off was simple and elegant: OM would specialize in breakthrough research, while Oticon stuck to incremental improvements. 'Hearing aids are more evolution – we are revolution. There is a difference between making a Tesla, and "just another Volkswagen". We are in a market where we're the smallest and we have to get in and grow,' an OM manager explained.

In the hearing aid industry, competition has inspired a rapid technology race. The development cycle is longer for implants than for hearing aids because the technique for surgical implanting is also part of the development challenge. 'We are not coming up with another hearing aid, like a well-oiled machine. We make prototypes we've never made before,' said an OM manager.

OM's initial focus was on bone-anchored hearing implants. It launched its first product in 2009. After acquiring the cochlear implant company Neurelec, OM launched its first cochlear implant in 2013.

OM's development focus is on 'projects'. Innovation is sought through cooperation with research units in hospitals, focus groups with users, and individuals. Other sources of innovation are about 100 R&D projects at varying stages of maturity that OM is involved in at universities and hospitals.

OM now operates in Gothenburg (bone-anchored implants), Nice (the cochlear implant) and Copenhagen (development of the processor for both bone-anchored and cochlear implants). The Copenhagen headquarters are in the same building as WDH and Oticon, and access to operational and distribution functions, and the Eriksholm research unit, is shared with Oticon.

These cross-boundary divisions made sense practically, but some staffers believed they also made creative collaboration a lot tougher. 'It is much more difficult to run with an idea,' said an OM employee. 'Who do I contact? The people I need to ask for things, to work on a new or different project might be in Poland. That's not easy.'

Another manager said structure was being driven by multi-site development: 'We have different countries, and must manage across them. So we've rolled out an organization that is multi-site. This also means that we have to be a bit more structured in the way we innovate between the sites.'

The development model is implemented in a matrix organization for a multi-site R&D function, to strengthen the bridge between new research and technology, and product development.

Both companies see constant innovation as essential, in their respective marketplaces, but their organizational designs reflect different cultures and innovation strategies. OM employees take on various tasks and can manage their own time.

There are few management layers at OM, and good communication about roadmaps and strategies makes it easy to prioritize issues and get all employees to take responsibility and make decisions. 'In the end it's about empowerment to make the right decisions. I trust my employees and give them a large amount of freedom,' said a manager. 'I feel I'm trusted when the top management informs me about their plans. That affects the decisions I make,' explained an OM employee.

The other advantage of OM is its size. OM is smaller. Employees say this allows them to work informally, with more initiative and accountability. 'Oticon's much bigger. It would take 15 years to develop a product I develop here in two years because of all their processes. Things move faster at OM and I have more room to decide for myself,' said an OM employee.

With dedicated research units and encouragement of innovation at an individual level through its reward schemes, Oticon separates research and workplace innovation. At OM, in contrast, external R&D partners function as structurally separate research units where more contextual support is given to employees, to balance their time between novel and incremental innovation.

Many OM employees are ex-Oticon, but management is aware that the new Oticon is very different from the old. 'It is not an automatic qualification to come from Oticon,' said one executive. 'Things are different here, so we need a different culture, to do it the way we do. If we get too many from Oticon, we could take in too much Oticon culture.'

A tale of two cultures

Today, the lower ranks at Oticon find it harder to get the time and support for innovative activity in their work, although there is a clear desire to do so.

One Oticon employee said that, although Oticon as a whole was innovative, 'I'm not innovative. I don't have the possibility for it in my work. My work is making small adjustments . . .' Another was not a great fan of Oticon's attempts to motivate people to be innovative through its Inventors Cube programme, an annual innovation contest. 'Cubes? They're actually demotivating. It's mainly for engineers. It would be nice if there were challenges for people who aren't engineers, or less technical. The focus is on technical advance, not on people wearing the hearing aid, or the audiologist fitting it.'

Size and the separation of innovation from day-to-day work at Oticon pose formidable communication challenges. 'There are lots of names for new initiatives in this organization,' said an Oticon employee. 'To be honest, I don't really focus on that very much.'

Another said: 'How things are done here, or how processes are run, is never clearly explained. I search on the intranet, but struggle to find information easily.'

An Oticon manager said: 'We have all these initiatives. We're really good at starting them, but we are not good at running them, or taking stock of them and trying to change what doesn't work. We kind of just let them die. We should go back and learn whether we really changed anything. It is the same with all the matrix stuff going on at the moment. I do not really see what it achieves. I am not sure how it is winning hearts and minds every day.'

Two researchers, Kirkeby and Foss, also found a marked difference in motivation between Oticon and OM, where entrepreneurialism is more embedded in the daily work. (9.3) The motivations of OM employees tended to be more altruistic than those of Oticon. 'I could not make a cooler product,' said one OM employee. 'I help deaf people get their hearing back and achieve a different life.'

One Oticon employee regretted the detachment of the innovation process from hearing aid customers: 'We have forgotten the user in all the technology. Stop and think. What would I do if I used a hearing aid? We think traditionally – that hearing aids need to be smaller and faster.'

An obvious way to interpret such organizational and cultural differences is to see Oticon as the more 'mature' organization and to predict, if only by implication, that OM will begin to resemble Oticon more closely as it matures and grows.

But another way of looking at this is to suppose the problem with the Kolind vision was not that it was too radical, but that it was too early. The idea of a decentralized organization where the agency resides in small, highly-motivated, self-organizing teams is not so eccentric in our fast-moving world as it might have seemed in the early 1990s.

Organizing work

One key advantage of every successful start-up is the small, tight-knit team that gets the business off the ground. Companies lose that special energy as they grow. Over time, that small, multi-functional team is replaced by armies of specialists who work through minutely choreographed processes. Recovering that energy and enthusiasm again is a key aspect of re-entrepreneuring. One way some companies have learned to meet this challenge is through a new kind of organizational principle we call 'light footprint management'. (9.4)

In a light footprint configuration, fewer people are brought together to do higher value-added work. Each is trained in a number of skills, and works in a small, autonomous team. Together, these team members possess most of the skills needed to execute whatever tasks they are assigned. They are self-adjusting, self-directed and self-improving.

Although not directed by the centre each team is aware of its internal and external customers and suppliers, and takes pains to establish and maintain mutually advantageous relationships with each of them, and with the organization as a whole.

Companies structured in such a modular way react more quickly to opportunities or threats, squander fewer resources and are more adaptable and innovative than conventional companies. They tend to be better attuned to the needs and desires of clients and customers, and better at collaborating with other companies or individuals.

The principles of re-entrepreneuring

The entrepreneurial spirit is so protean even in its re-entrepreneuring guise that it might seem impossible to draw any conclusions about it, let alone a set of principles. Yet as we thought this over and considered these cases, we started to see certain patterns, and felt that we actually could draw some conclusions. Although there are certainly more useful insights where these came from, these five were the ones that struck us as most useful.

1 The DNA of an organization carries the seeds of the future

There's a heady rush of energy at the time a company is created. The founder, powered by his own adrenalin rush, injects an infectious enthusiasm and DNA into the company, which inspires everyone to act. No idea is too big to be pursued. This is a time to break out of the paradigms of conventional thinking. This is not a time for safe, calculated risks. This is a time to think big.

Over time, as an organization matures, this tempo slows down. Slowly, the organization settles down into business-as-usual. The entrepreneurial spark goes cold. The company starts to make safer bets, it starts to operate within fixed paradigms and the confines of its current business model, employees switch to the managerial mode and for a while, blue-sky thinking becomes a thing of the past and the company gets stuck in a rut.

What companies forget is that the entrepreneurial spark is not something needed only at the start of the company. It is something that the founder embedded in the DNA and can be invoked again to re-energize the company. If you look at companies with long histories, very often you can see how the entrepreneurial genes embedded by the company's founder have been invoked time and again to help the company adapt and even become a new version of itself. Apple would have always been a personal computer company if the entrepreneurial energy embedded by Steve Jobs forever lay dormant within it. This is what accounts for the 'uniqueness' of a company in the long run. A company's DNA has nothing to do with the products it develops, or the sector it operates in. The DNA boils down to its very purpose. Entrepreneurial energy is constantly nurtured by the DNA. It also inspires the manner in which things are done and objectives are achieved – what we could normally call the operating style. The DNA is central to re-entrepreneuring.

2 The right triggers can rekindle the latent entrepreneurial spirit

Most organizations view disruptions as setbacks and view them negatively. But if handled well, disruptions – that often come in the form of mergers and acquisitions and restructuring or technological changes – can be leveraged as opportunities to press the reset button. These are, in a sense, opportunities to look at the company from a fresh and unencumbered perspective – pretty much like the founder viewed the company at the time of its birth. As we saw in the bibliotheca–3M case, a merger can be an opportunity to start from a clean slate and think entrepreneurially.

More generally, a time of crisis usually brings the company to face the option of death or disruption; this is usually when the company is the most ready for re-entrepreneuring.

3 Re-entrepreneuring is part of staying relevant

Re-entrepreneuring does not take anything for granted. As a result, the factors that keep an organization anchored in the status quo are not viewed as constraints. As a result, re-entrepreneuring is able to unleash fresh thinking and help an organization stay relevant in our fast-changing environment. It is what has helped organizations with long histories – like TUI or Deutsche Post – adapt to the changing times. That is not to say that re-entrepreneuring is only for organizations with long histories. For younger organizations like BGI and Didi Chuxing, re-entrepreneuring is a 'habit'. It is something they do frequently to stay competitive and always be ahead of the pack. They view everything through a different lens – from how to tap new opportunities to the mundane aspects of managing a company.

4 Simply adding 'entrepreneurship' does not help; it has to be blended with the 'Re'

A lot of organizations believe that in order to get out of the rut, they can simply hire entrepreneurial people, create skunkworks or launch corporate ventures, and poof! Somehow the magic will happen. They are mistaken. Adding entrepreneurship on top is, at best, like a

Band-aid and will not lead to lasting change. Any new initiatives that come out of adding entrepreneurship will not be able to assimilate into the company and become mainstream.

Re-entrepreneuring has to come from within. In order to work, the entrepreneurial streak has to be combined with the existing culture, capabilities, characteristics and assets of the organization. In this way, re-entrepreneuring does not discard the legacies and traditions a company has acquired over time. It makes use of what is relevant, builds upon it and makes it ready for the future.

5 Entrepreneurship must be fostered while being protected from the day-to-day grind of managing a company

At the end of the day, entrepreneurship and managing require two very different mindsets. Most entrepreneurs like to do what they do best: give shape and form to new ideas and translate them into reality. (9.5) Encumbering them with the day-to-day business of running the company is a huge mistake. It will focus their energies on activities that they are not particularly interested in and leave them with little time to focus on what they ought to. That is often why many entrepreneurs make 'not the best' managers.

Which is why, it sometimes makes sense to separate entrepreneurship from managing. In the case of Wargaming, the online gaming company, if the founder Victor Kislyi had taken the onus of day-to-day administration and managing upon him, today Wargaming would have been a very different animal. Its success today, to a large extent, is due to the conscious separation of the two activities.

Summing up

The entrepreneurial spirit is not just a distinctive characteristic of the start-up stage of an organization's lifecycle or the personality of a company's founder. It is not a set of personality traits, either, such as a predisposition for risk-taking or a preference for independence and self-determination. Instead, the entrepreneurial impulse is latent in all of us, and often just awaits the right situation or the right encouragement to bring it out. Even in an established company, simply nurturing this spirit can yield surprisingly profitable results.

The propensity to re-entrepreneur lurks in the background.

Discontinuities in an organization's development, such as acquisitions, mergers and privatizations, offer not-to-be-wasted opportunities to make a fresh start, a chance to reset an organization's development clock by resetting its habits, attitudes, culture and mission. As Rahm Emanuel, the chief of staff in the first Obama Administration and current mayor of Chicago, once said, 'You never want to let a serious crisis go to waste . . . It's an opportunity to do things you think you could not do before.' For the 3M Library Systems side of the 3M–bibliotheca merger, for instance, its acquisition by a younger, hungrier company freed a lot of creative energy and determination that had been pent up by its famous parent.

Re-entrepreneuring focuses on adaptation, not optimization. It deduces the health of the organization not only from its profit and loss statement, but from how well its business model appears to suit its environment.

Many believe that the entrepreneurial instinct is the sole preserve of the public sector. That is incorrect. The adoption of an entrepreneurial outlook can also help state-owned monopolies and government departments adapt to changing environments or priorities.

In future, re-entrepreneuring will become vital to the health of a company. In industries characterized by rapid, and disruptive, technological advances, only the entrepreneurial will survive. In such industries – and, increasingly, most industries answer to that description – survival depends not on efficiency alone, but on efficient novelty. In less disruptive industries, re-entrepreneuring will become a crucial competitive advantage.

Organizations that remain open-minded about what they are and what they do and stay on the lookout for signals heralding changes in their marketplaces – and the opportunities and threats that accompany them – will gain competitive advantages over their less adaptable and far-seeing rivals.

10

Epilogue

In 2014, we at Roland Berger launched something called Terra Numerata. A digital business platform, Terra Numerata is our attempt to plant the seeds of a European 'Digital Valley'. It is a platform that is meant to bring together companies from different industries and help them form alliances and push digital innovation.

They say that innovation happens at the intersections of disciplines. That is exactly what we are trying to do here. By bringing together a diverse set of companies, start-ups, incubators, investors and experts, we hope we could spark off interesting new exchanges that would potentially lead to new ideas and, hopefully, new business models.

But to achieve this ambition, we had to break out of our traditional paradigms. If Terra Numerata was to succeed, it needed to be based on an open architecture framework. Rather than us trying to control everything, we had to create an appealing proposition which would attract the right people and companies. Instead of adopting rigid top-down structures, we decided to go for an ecosystems approach. That way, interested parties could come together of their own accord and create much more value than they would have in a controlled environment.

Today, Terra Numerata is a resounding success. It has evolved into a global network of more than 40 core partners, including start-ups, accelerators, incubators, investors, data scientists, design thinking agencies, prototypers, developers, IoT experts, communication agencies, digital communities and recruiters.

Many inspiring business stories found their starting point in Terra Numerata. For instance, Roland Berger partnered with Dataiku, the New York-based software company, developing collaborative data science software, enabling our consultants to achieve more complex data analysis. For the mobile operator Zain, we were able to propose an innovative segmentation of their customer databases, and a platform offering the most adapted offer to a client according to his or her consumption pattern.

Through Terra Numerata, consultants are enriched with technical tools and skills which are essential in today's world (and would be too costly to develop in-house) while consolidating the core business of consulting: bringing knowledge with high added value for the customer. This is a typical example of re-entrepreneuring.

Another example from Terra Numerata would be of how the start-up accelerator Numa and Roland Berger teamed up to help the French oil and gas company Total to build its own start-up studio. The goal for Total was to accelerate its digital transformation, develop new projects and help create new business lines and future sources of revenue. One outcome from this was the platform Clean, which is now the leading online car washing brand in France.

As a traditional consulting company, spawning a European 'Digital Valley' is a lofty goal and probably not our business. Why then, you might ask, would we do something like that?

The answers lie in some introspection we did in 2013. That was a rather tumultuous period for us. Our former CEO tried to sell the company. Roland Berger had many suitors, but eventually we decided that we wanted to stay independent.

It was a risky bet. By the end of 2013, things looked bleak. We had lost the pride we had in our past, and the confidence we had in our future. People wanted to leave the company and clients, the mainstay of the consulting business, had serious doubts about our future prospects.

The trend at that time was for consulting companies to merge with the big players. In choosing to stay independent, we ended up putting a lot of pressure on ourselves. We had to not just survive, but we also had to break out of the mould: we had to be more than a classical consulting company. We had to find new ways to unlock value while also dealing with the short-term problem of ensuring survival.

So in 2014, we embarked on our own journey of re-entrepreneuring and became the new Roland Berger. That did not mean that we abandoned everything we believed in. We went back to our roots. We retained the traditions instilled by our founder. But we also looked at the future. We realized that innovation would pave the way to a future that lay in new opportunities like digital and artificial intelligence. We also realized that there might be new ways of doing things. We applied fully the principles of re-entrepreneuring to ourselves.

So we stepped into the future with our new brand (what we call the 'titanium B') and with a lot of new initiatives – Terra Numerata was just one of them. We started advocating new approaches to our clients – such as light footprint management, which called for the adoption of modular, adaptive and agile business models. Additionally, we took a long, hard look at every line of business and engaged in an entrepreneurial restructuring exercise, shaving off excess costs in the process.

We also changed the way we ourselves operated. We took a hard look at our traditional values and came up with something we call the '10 Commitments', a mix of the values embedded in the company by our founder and values more attuned with today's realities. We rejuvenated our partner group with more than half our partners being new. By doing this, we could break out of our older mental models and instil fresh thinking in the company. We changed the format of our partner meetings and made them more participative to allow for ideas to fly around freely. We also balanced the traditional Roland Berger construct by enlarging our focus on emerging regions like Asia.

Today, we are just as strong in traditional consulting as in new domains like digital business and artificial intelligence. We have gained tremendous ground in Asia, particularly China. In 2018 we are doing our best year ever both in top-line and in bottom-line growth. We have more than recovered from 2013–2014, easily the toughest time in our 50-year history.

That is the magic of re-entrepreneuring. Our 50-year-old values and principles remain unchanged, and yet we are in tune with the changing times.

The re-entrepreneuring exercise we went through infused a new spirit among the partners. The air was thick with new ideas and there was a palpable sense of enthusiasm and the momentum to take things through. That rejuvenated the company. We remain entrepreneurial and innovative. We remain relevant. And we became a 'young old' company.

What you read in this book is not about abstract models or constructs that sound good in theory but fail miserably in practice. This is about real cases and real results. Re-entrepreneuring works. We have experienced it first-hand.

We live in an 'age of dizzying acceleration'. (10.1) It is hard to make sense of the world when everything around us is always in a state of flux. Business models need to be adaptable to new realities, shifting paradigms and entire environments that change overnight.

In the past 50 years, dramatic changes have broadened, broken and reformed the business landscape The next 50 years promise to be even more dramatic, with waves of change that are likely to be stronger and more frequent than they have been in the past. As Thomas Friedman puts it, the planet's 'three largest forces – Moore's law (technology), the Market (globalization), and Mother Nature (climate change and biodiversity loss) – are accelerating all at once'. Organizations no longer have the liberty to peacefully mull over how they need to respond to these changing realities.

The certainty of dramatic change, combined with a fundamental uncertainty about the forms it might take or where it might lead, is the modern organization's main adaptive challenge. If you cannot know what will happen, how can you prepare for it?

Our answer is to build for flexibility, to take nothing for granted, and to react quickly to each threat or opportunity that presents itself by re-entrepreneuring your capabilities and assets. We believe that in the current times where the word 'disruption' is on everyone's lips and things are moving at breakneck speed, it is imperative for organizations to start re-entrepreneuring themselves. We have done it and so can you. Join us in that journey.

NOTES

Chapter 1

1 The concept of 'excubator' is a good alternative to develop disruptive innovation, while keeping it 'at hand' for the company. It combines the operating system of a lab or an incubator with outward-looking investment logic, aiming at a quick go-to-market test. But this solution is not very widespread, especially in Europe.

Chapter 4

1 The duration of the payment depended on the age of the recipient and the time of former employment with liability for social insurance. For a person younger than 50, the unemployment benefit is now limited to 12 months. For people above 50, it can be paid for up to 24 months, depending on how long they were employed before. (Source: Bundesagentur für Arbeit, Nuremberg, Germany)

2 December 2017, Eurostat, Bureau of Labor Statistics

Chapter 7

1 This is what Charles-Edouard Bouée has theorized under the 'Light Footprint Strategy' concept. Or how, in chaotic environments, companies should adopt agile structures, both centralized (for core functions) and decentralized (with autonomous teams operating on the field), to stay close to their markets. (*Light Footprint Management: Leadership in Times of Change*, London: Bloomsbury, 2013)

SOURCES

Preface

0.1 Charles-Edouard Bouée, *Light Footprint Management: Leadership in Times of Change*, London: Bloomsbury, 2013.

Introduction

0.2 Alfred D. Chandler, Jr., *The Visible Hand: The Managerial Revolution in American Business*, Cambridge, MA: Harvard University Press, 1977.

0.3 *Prime Mover of Progress*, London: The Institute of Economic Affairs, 1980.

Chapter 1

1.1 *Inc. Howard Stevenson*, see https://www.inc.com/eric-schurenberg/the-best-definition-of-entepreneurship.html

1.2 The material on Apple is mostly from Walter Isaacson, *Steve Jobs*, London: Little, Brown, 2011.

1.3 Vijay Govindarajan and Anup Srivastava, 'Strategy when Creative Destruction Accelerates', Tuck School of Business Working Paper No. 2836135, 7th September 2016. Available at SSRN: https://ssrn.com/abstract=2836135

1.4 Jacques Monod, *Chance and Necessity: An Essay on the Natural Philosophy of Modern Biology*, New York: Alfred A. Knopf, 1971.

Chapter 2

2.1   http://www.post-und-telekommunikation.de/PuT/1Fundus/Dokumente/
      Geschaeftsberichte/Deutsche%20Post/1994-GB-DBP-Postdienst.pdf
2.2   http://www.dpdhl.com/de/ueber_uns/geschichte.html

Chapter 3

3.1   https://media.ford.com/content/fordmedia/feu/en/news/2016/02/03/
      ford-accelerates-transformation-plan-in-europe-to-build-vibrant-.html
3.2   http://www.spiegel.de/international/business/q-cells-bankruptcy-heralds-
      end-of-german-solar-cell-industry-a-825490.html
3.3   http://veranstaltungen.handelsblatt.com/restrukturierung/sma-solar-
      technology-zurueck-auf-der-erfolgsspur/
3.4   https://www.autoblog.com/2016/02/06/ford-europe-layoffs-official/

Chapter 4

4.1   http://www.spiegel.de/international/business/laser-optics-in-jena-a-bright-
      light-in-eastern-germany-a–656416.html and https://www.jenoptik.com/
      investors/at-a-glance
4.2   See http://doku.iab.de/veranstaltungen/2005/Samf_2005_eichhorst_folien.
      pdf and the book by Hendrik Meyer, *Was kann der Staat? Eine Analyse
      der rot-grünen Reformen in der Sozialpolitik*, Bielefeld: Transcipt Verlag,
      p. 158.
4.3   *Financial Times*, 7th January 2018.

Chapter 5

5.1   https://www.fastcompany.com/3014992/pixars-john-lasseter-on-steve-
      jobs-creativity-and-disney-infinity

5.2   http://geschichte.salzgitter-ag.com/fileadmin/mediadb/microsites/
      geschichte/geschichte_unternehmensbereiche/unternehmensbereich_
      energie/mannesmann-geschichte/Mannesmann_Geschichte_D__
      Stand_2015_09_16.pdf

5.3   https://www.salzgitter-ag.com/de/konzern/geschaeftsbereiche/
      mannesmann.html

5.4   https://www.vodafone.de/unternehmen/meilensteine.html

5.5   http://www.manager-magazin.de/finanzen/artikel/a–92911.html

5.6   http://www.spiegel.de/wirtschaft/otelo-mannesmann-arcor-kauft-
      festnetz-a–15637.html

5.7   https://www.heise.de/newsticker/meldung/Arcor-ist-Geschichte–749301.
      html

5.8   http://www.spiegel.de/wirtschaft/atecs-mannesmann-gent-gibt-siemens-
      bosch-den-zuschlag-a–72972.html

5.9   https://hbr.org/2016/07/wpps-ceo-on-turning-a-portfolio-of-companies-
      into-a-growth-machine

Chapter 6

6.1   Benjamin Shobert, 'Meet The Chinese Company that Wants to be the Intel
      of personalized medicine', *Forbes*, 18th January 2017.

6.2   http://www.statisticbrain.com/average-historic-price-of-ram/

6.3   Neelima Mahajan, 'Genetics Research: Decoding BGI's genes', *CKGSB
      Knowledge*, 20th January 2014. http://knowledge.ckgsb.edu.cn/2014/01/20/
      technology/genetics-research-decoding-bgis-genes/

6.4   https://www.wired.com/2017/05/chinese-genome-giant-sets-sights-
      uitimate-sequencer/

Chapter 7

7.1   'Secretive Billionaire Reveals How He Toppled Apple in China', *Bloomberg
      News*, 19th March 2017.

7.2   Brad Stone and Lulu Yilun Chen, 'Uber Slayer: How China's Didi beat the
      ride-hailing superpower', *Bloomberg Businessweek*, 6th October 2016.
      https://www.forbes.com/sites/zackfriedman/2017/05/30/tech-
      unicorns/#24cd61891179

Chapter 8

8.1 'Entrepreneurship: A working definition', *Harvard Business Review*, 10th January 2013.

Chapter 9

9.1 *N is for Navigating*, a presentation by Bill Fischer, IMD Business School, 2014.

9.2 *Fast Company*, June–July, 1996.

9.3 Mathilde Fog Kirkeby and Nicolai Foss, *The Multidextrous Organization: Learning from the William Demant Holding Experience*, unpublished working paper, 2017.

9.4 Charles-Edouard Bouée, *Light Footprint Management: Leadership in Times of Change*, London: Bloomsbury, 2013.

9.5 Fiona Cannon with Nicky Elford, *The Agility Mindset: How Reframing Flexible Working Delivers Competitive Advantage*, London: Palgrave Macmillan, 2017.

Chapter 10

10.1 Hartmut Rosa, *Social Acceleration*, Columbia, OH: Columbia University Press, 2015.

INDEX